SpringerBriefs in Economics

More information about this series at http://www.springer.com/series/8876

Meenakshi Rajeev · B.P. Vani

Financial Access of the Urban Poor in India

A Story of Exclusion

Springer

Meenakshi Rajeev
Centre for Economic Studies and Policy (CESP)
Institute for Social and Economic Change (ISEC)
Bangalore
India

B.P. Vani
Centre for Economic Studies and Policy (CESP)
Institute for Social and Economic Change (ISEC)
Bangalore
India

ISSN 2191-5504 ISSN 2191-5512 (electronic)
SpringerBriefs in Economics
ISBN 978-81-322-3710-5 ISBN 978-81-322-3712-9 (eBook)
DOI 10.1007/978-81-322-3712-9

Library of Congress Control Number: 2016963305

Printed on acid-free paper

This Springer imprint is published by Springer Nature
The registered company is Springer (India) Pvt. Ltd.
The registered company address is: 7th Floor, Vijaya Building, 17 Barakhamba Road, New Delhi 110 001, India

Acknowledgements

This book is an outcome of our project on the same theme funded by CAFRAL, RBI, Mumbai. Subsequently, we have made appropriate modifications to capture the most recent developments. We thank CAFRAL and the Reserve Bank of India for their support. We also thank ISEC for its support during the period of this project.

Contents

About the Authors

Meenakshi Rajeev is the RBI Chair Professor at the Institute for Social and Economic Change, Bangalore, India. Having obtained her Ph.D. from the Indian Statistical Institute, Kolkata, Prof. Meenakshi has wide ranging publications in both national and international journals. Her recent book "Emerging Issues in Economics Development" has been published by Oxford University Press. Her earlier book "Estimating District Income in India" was published by Macmillan. She has served as visiting faculty in a number of universities in Europe and the USA. Her areas of interest include issues related to banking and credit, development economics (game theoretic modeling), industrial economics and labor relations.

B.P. Vani is Assistant Professor at the Centre for Economic Studies and Policy (CESP), Institute for Social and Economic Change, Bangalore, India. She holds a Masters degree in Statistics from Bangalore University. She has published papers in journals of international repute and her research focuses on poverty and income distribution.

Chapter 1
Introduction

Economic theory postulates that investment is the primary requisite for economic growth, and financial intermediaries play a significant role in the growth process as they function as necessary conduits for mobilizing savings and channelizing them as productive investments for economic growth. It is therefore imperative that easy access to financial services is ensured especially to the lower strata of the economic-pyramid for ensuring inclusive growth. Theory also talks about other channels through which benefits of financial intermediation transmit to generate economic growth. First, it is important for mobilization of much needed savings, which would remain untapped if the financial sector remained inaccessible to a large section of people. Secondly, the financial sector plays an important role in channelizing these resources towards productive endeavors of the population, both rich and poor. Importantly it can also improve productive efficiency and thereby enhance income. It also helps in human resource development as resources for education or skill development become available through credit from the financial sector. Therefore, access to formal financial intermediation needs to be made easy in order to enable the poor to reap the benefits of growth.

Amongst various roles that a financial intermediary can play, the role of credit is critical in a country where a large percentage of people are self employed either in agriculture or in small informal businesses. These small so called entrepreneurs are in regular need of funds at least for their working capital needs. In rural agriculture, farmers have somewhat better access to credit due to priority sector lending norms for agriculture. But the informal small businesses especially in urban regions are particularly deprived of any source of funds. To provide credit facilities to the poorer sections of the economy, who are usually excluded from the system, financial inclusion drive is critical (Rajeev 2015). Credit facilities in India come from different sources, which can be broadly classified as formal and informal, and the terms and conditions of credit normally vary with its source. It is therefore important that these credit starved sections are brought under the canopy of

This book is an outcome of our project on the same theme funded by CAFRAL, RBI, Mumbai. Subsequently, we have made appropriate modifications to capture the most recent developments. We thank CAFRAL and the Reserve Bank of India for their support. Usual disclaimer applies.

M. Rajeev and B.P. Vani, *Financial Access of the Urban Poor in India*,
SpringerBriefs in Economics, DOI 10.1007/978-81-322-3712-9_1

formal financial services of the economy in order to ensure provision and timely disbursal of loans, extending services such as insurance, financial counseling etc. at affordable costs. Financial inclusion, according to the Finance Minister's budget speech, is defined as "the process of ensuring access to timely and adequate credit and financial services to vulnerable groups at an affordable cost" (Union Budget 2007–2008). The outcome of financial inclusion is not only recognized as pro-poor but also pro-growth. It is seen as an instrument that would involve and enable each citizen of a country to use financial services and improve her/his future, thereby adding to the country's progress through benefitting both at the supply as well as the demand end. On the one hand, it facilitates banks to expand their operation and increase their services, and on the other, affords people living in remote areas accessibility to banking services at lower transaction costs.

Recognising the importance of financial inclusion as one of the contributing factors in inclusive growth, steps are being taken by the financial regulators, governments and banking industry to make the financial system more inclusive. The significant initiatives taken by the Reserve Bank of India and the Indian banking sector include adoption of business correspondent model, introducing "no-frills account" and issuing "General credit cards" for low deposits and credits.

With a view to promote financial literacy and familiarise financial services among rural areas, RBI formulated a model scheme for Financial Literacy and Credit Counselling Centres (FLCCCs) and advised lead banks to open a FLCCC in their respective districts. To reduce operating cost of providing banking services, innovative measures like e-payments, mobile banking, and electronic benefit transfers (EBT), introducing handheld guidance like business correspondent models, opening bank branches and ATMs in remote areas etc. are also undertaken by banks under RBI mandate. Alternate financial institutions such as micro-finance institutions and Self-Help Groups are also being promoted in order to reach financial services to the excluded.

One major initiative taken by the Government is the "Pradhan Mantri Jan Dhan Yojana". The honourable Prime Minister of India Mr Modi announced this scheme on his first Independence Day speech on 15 August, 2014. The scheme covers both rural and urban areas and provides several benefits to the account holders which include over draft facility, accident and life insurance benefits and so on.

While acknowledging the role of such instruments, it needs to be recognised that the drive was initially (during the last decade) rural centric and large number of rural accounts were opened under the drive. Subsequently if we look at the Jan Dhan Yojana, number of accounts open in the rural areas (as of July 2016) is around 14 crores is much higher than the number of accounts opened in the urban regions, i.e. 9 crores. Though this may be partly due to demand side factors pertaining to the urban regions of India, one needs to recognise that the problem of financial exclusion exists not only in rural regions but also in urban areas. While the financial inclusion of the rural poor especially farmers have been well discussed, financial exclusion of the urban poor has not yet received the academic attention it deserves (Rajeev 2015). The challenges of financial inclusion and accessibility in the urban areas are quite different from those found in the rural regions where (i.e., in urban regions) the possibility of physical access to financial services is much higher. Despite having innumerable branches of private and public sector banks, a majority of disadvantaged and low income groups are yet to fully utilize banking services in urban areas. According to 2010 census, 31% of the Indian population lives in urban areas, and it is estimated to reach 40% by 2030. With increasing urbanisation, there is also an increase in the number of urban poor, and the latest NSSO report reveals that there are over 80 million poor people living in the cities and towns of India. A vast majority of them are migrants and workers engaged in the unorganized sector, and are socio-economically and geographically disadvantaged. And it is this group of the urban population who lack accessibility to financial products and services like savings, credit, insurance, remittances etc. and hence depend on informal savings and credit systems to meet their personal, health, and livelihood-related needs. Unsurprisingly, they struggle to repay such borrowings, which further impede their ability to escape the cycle of poverty. Another major group that this book is going to address is the self employed households. A large percentage of urban poor are self employed and engaged in small businesses as street vendors, small service providers and so on. These groups of people, being engaged in business, are in regular needs of funds. While they may have got financially included by opening a bank account under some scheme, they still lack the most necessary service, viz., the access to credit from the formal sources.

Some of the factors that have been keeping urban poor and migrant workers unbanked are their low, irregular earnings and procedural complications. Since they are mostly employed in unorganised sectors, and keep moving from one city to another in search of better work opportunities, they are seldom able to produce the documentation required to get formal banking facilities. Further, asymmetric information, bigger family size, lack of financial literacy and consequent poor money management capability, etc., forbid them from formal banking services, and hence they prefer to keep their savings at home or participate in informal saving schemes like chit fund.

The urban self employed households on the other hand usually are not engaged in migratory works and as this study finds are also earning reasonable income. As mentioned, the most essential service for such urban self employed, which is the focus group of this research, is access to credit and their lack of access is often due to their inability to provide any kind of security or deal with the procedural complications.

According to a planning commission report (2011. See http://planningcommission.nic.in/hackathon/Urban_Development.pdf), there are three concerns involved in the provision of banking and financial services to urban poor. Firstly, creating better banking infrastructure in urban areas alone does not guarantee banking access to urban poor. Secondly, credit from commercial banks to small and micro enterprises is not forthcoming and in fact it has declined from 15.2% in 1994–95 to 6.6% in 2007–08, but this decline has not been calculated separately for urban areas. Thirdly, in the absence of national level data on access of urban poor to banking and financial services in India as also on the initiatives of the RBI in this direction, it is difficult to

Table 1.1 Incidence of indebtedness: all India

Rural		Urban	
MPCE	India	MPCE	India
0–254	23.15	0–384	18.36
254–338	25.04	384–511	18.23
338–425	26.29	511–600	19.13
425–510	27.48	600–700	18.22
510–600	27.11	700–800	16.61
600–700	29.20	800–950	17.95
700–950	28.80	950–1500	16.57
950–1500	26.28	1500–2500	19.32
1500–3000	29.53	2500–3500	20.14
Above 3000	16.85	Above 3500	15.36
Total	26.54	Total	17.79

MPCE Monthly Per capita Consumption Expenditure
Source Authors' analysis of NSSO 59th round data

arrive at any meaningful conclusion on the matter of urban poor's access to banking finance in India. Thus the lack of statistics adversely impacts policy making for this group.

In the absence of other statistical data, the only option was the NSSO 59th round (All India Debt and Investment Survey 2005) which provided substantial information regarding household debt and investment for 1,43,285 households in India, covering both rural and urban areas. Subsequently, NSSO 70th round data for the period 2012-13 on the subject became available. Notably, there has been very few studies that came up with rigorous unit level analysis of this household level data. A quick analysis of NSSO data shows that access to credit, as indicated through incidence of indebtedness[1] is lower in urban areas than in rural areas (Table 1.1). When only the farmer households are considered, then access to credit increases to 50% (about 50% of the farmer households have been able to take loan) and this also shows rural–urban differences in access to credit, which is one of the important indicators of accessibility to financial services.

Currently, there are several insightful studies on rural credit market, especially in relation to farmer households (see NABARD 2001; Mohan 2004). Though it is hypothesized that access to credit is rather low even for self-employed households in the urban regions, there have not been enough studies to unravel this phenomenon. Therefore, there is an urgent need to find answers to the following question: What are the problems faced by an urban self employed person/establishment in accessing formal banking network for deposit, credit and other needs? Within the

[1]Incidence of Indebtedness is defined as the percentage of households belonging to a category such as income groups etc., having outstanding loan on the date of survey to the total number of households in that category and we argue can be considered as an indication for accessibility to credit.

urban region, while the problem of credit for small manufacturing industries sector has been studied to some extent, the problems of services sector, especially trading activities, where vast majority of people seek employment have not yet received the academic attention it deserves.

The ways to tackle the problem of exclusion also differ between rural and urban regions. In the context of the urban poor, mobile banking services along with appropriate technologies—biometrics and handheld collection devices—can be low cost solutions to reach potential clients within limited geographical areas such as trading market areas. In such areas in urban regions a large segment of clients can be tapped, which may not be possible in a rural setup. However, the role of personal interactions in customer outreach cannot be under-estimated. As urban formal banks are overcrowded with educated middle class population, poor develops a psychological barriers to access services in such an environment. One of the issues revealed during our initial interactions with trader-borrowers is that while an informal lender personally collects repayment amount on a regular basis through individual visits, banks do not pursue repayment so regularly. Consequently borrowers tend to be lethargic and finally face default with large dues. In addition to alerts through mobile phones or use of business correspondents in a local kiosk based set up can be possible solutions to such problems, and induction of such innovative methods can reduce the cost of availing services. Cost here not only includes rate of interest but also the cost incurred by the borrower in availing the service, which includes time cost, opportunity cost and other transaction costs such as travel costs. Therefore, the formal financial institutions should extend coverage and deliver their products keeping in view the specific needs of the urban poor and create innovative financial services to attract and induce households and enterprises to seek banking services.

In this backdrop, this study focuses on the issue of financial exclusion with particular reference to the self employed urban population in India. In order to provide a macro perspective at the outset, the study begins with an analysis of the nature and extent of urban indebtedness in India, based on NSSO 59th and 70th round data; the latter is the latest household based macro level data available on indebtedness. Further, based on a primary survey conducted in Karnataka (Bengaluru and Tumkur districts) of self employed persons engaged in the services sector, this research attempts to understand the following issues: The nature and extent of financial exclusion of different self employed persons/services establishments, classifying them in terms of extent of their inclusion, such as completely excluded, partially excluded and fully included. This necessitates preparation of a complete list of possible services such as deposit, credit, insurance, remittances and others desirable for the population under consideration. The reasons for financial exclusion and how do they currently meet their financial needs for different purposes, and under what terms and conditions are important issues to be understood. We also ask what can be possible interventions to improve the extent of use of financial services?

In this backdrop, the book unfolds in the following way: The next chapter provides a brief review of literature which highlights the importance of financial inclusion (FI) for reduction of poverty and enhancement of growth and development, and essential infrastructure required for carrying out an effective FI programmes.

The problem of financial exclusion is not faced by India alone. Many developing and emerging nations have faced the challenges of providing an inclusive financial infrastructure, and some interesting experiences from the countries across the globe are presented in Chap. 3.

Concentrating on India we next present a macro perspective with a micro foundation. One of the primary aims of financial inclusion in India is to provide necessary resources through credit to the poor by means of formal financial sector to meet their needs for income generating as well as consumption activities such as on health or education. One of the major sources of information regarding accessibility to credit and other financial services by the households of different income (expenditure) categories is the national sample survey organisation (NSSO) data. Chapter 4 analyses NSSO debt and investment survey (59th and 70th rounds) data to understand the nature and extent of accessibility to credit by different sections of people, classified according to various income and social categories. This exercise provides us inputs regarding the kind of prioritised attention needed by different economic and social classes in the urban regions of the country. NSSO data however does not provide information regarding the problems of the poor and possible solutions. A detailed survey based analysis therefore seeks go deeper to capture some of these issues.

While Chap. 5 describes the survey methods and sample regions, basic characteristics of sample observations are presented in Chap. 6. Chapter 7 provides a detailed analysis of data on the level of financial inclusion and its determinants. The concluding chapter follows thereafter.

References

National Sample Survey Organization (NSSO) (2005). All India debt and investment survey, NSSO, New Delhi

Mohan R (2004) Agricultural credit in India: status, issues and future agenda. RBI, Bulletin, November

NABARD (2001) Report of the expert committee on rural credit. Chairman Dr. V.S. Vyas

Rajeev M (2015) Urban financial exclusion: a neglected concern. The Financial Express

Chapter 2
A Brief Review of Literature

The literature that forms the backdrop of the study has mainly focused on issues revolving around the importance of financial inclusion and various challenges associated with it together with measures to tackle the problems.[1] The issues related to financial inclusion include availability of physical and financial infrastructure to provide accessibility to banking, technological and technical innovations to reduce transaction costs, and financial literacy to reduce the problem of information asymmetry and the problem of market imperfection in financial services.

2.1 Theoretical Argument for Financial Inclusion

Focusing on the importance of financial intermediation for different agents of an economy, Subbarao (2013) highlights that it provides opportunity for the poor to improve their incomes and quality of life. For the suppliers of the services viz., the banks, it provides steady low cost savings. State can also benefit from financial inclusion as it helps to better channelization of funds and thereby reduce poverty. All these aspects make FI good for the economy as a whole.

2.1.1 Financial Intermediation and Information Asymmetry

If the markets are perfectly competitive, characterized by perfect information, financial intermediation acts more like a veil and its role therefore cannot be considered as substantive. Over time however, it has been recognized that information asymmetry and moral hazard problems are integral parts of financial markets. This gave rise to theories that highlight the role of financial sector in

[1]See also Schumpeter (1934) of a braoder discussion on development.

M. Rajeev and B.P. Vani, *Financial Access of the Urban Poor in India*,
SpringerBriefs in Economics, DOI 10.1007/978-81-322-3712-9_2

augmenting growth. A number of channels can be conceived as to show how the transmission may work (Theil 2001).[2]

2.1.2 Financial Intermediation and Growth

Growth theory tells us that investment is instrumental for economic growth and financial intermediaries play the crucial role of allocation of capital. Generally relation between financial sector and growth is studied theoretically by several authors (see Harrison et al. 1999). Therefore financial inclusion which provides access to financial services to all can be an essential tool to ensure that some sections of society are not deprived and capital is allocated to all sections of society.

2.1.2.1 Role of Savings

Well developed financial sector help bringing savings into the formal system and thereby can aid to gather resources for investments. Diamond and Dybvig (1983) consider financial institutions as ‘coalition of depositors’ who get the resources to be dispersed to the people in times of adversities, risks and thereby provide insurance cover. In developing countries where the poor saves through informal network often lose their money and a large amount of resources remain out of the formal financial system.

2.1.2.2 Improving Productivity and Efficiency

Financial intermediation helps to improve productivity and efficiency by a number of channels. As mentioned by Thiel (2001) by selecting profitable projects they help to improve their productivity further. Provision of liquidity and allocation of risks are other channels where productivity improvement and efficiency can take place.

In the context of developing nations it is observed by many that the poor are unable to use the basic necessary technology due to lack of funds and financial help can improve their productivity helping them to adopt such methods. In case of Indian agriculture NSSO data can be used to show that the farmers with credit have higher productivity than the non borrowers (see Rajeev 2011).

[2]Theil, Michael (2001) Finance and Economic Growth: A review of theory and the available evidences, European Communities, ECFINC3/469/01-EN, http://europa.eu.int/economy_finance.

2.1.2.3 Financial Intermediation and Human Resource Development

An accessible financial system can help the poor to access resources for education and thereby improve the human resources of a nation. Human resource development can help knowledge building and innovation leading to a situation of increasing returns and further enhance productivity and growth. The relation between human resource and growth has been well established in the growth theory literature (see Romer 1986, 1990). Galor and Zeira (1993) argue that the poor are unable to invest in human capital due to financial market imperfections (particularly due to high cost of borrowing) and therefore forced to continue in unskilled work which diminishes their lifetime earnings and that acts as a vicious cycle. Similarly, restrictions in occupational choice due to lack of education and training is highlighted by Banerjee and Newman (1993) through their model on credit market imperfections.

2.1.3 Policy Transmission Argument

Several policies especially such as monetary policy aims at impacting the economy through interventions in the money/credit market through financial intermediaries like banks. In particular, interventions of the Reserve Bank of India in terms of changing the repo rate, CRR etc. is frequently experienced in the Indian economy. But if half of the population is out of the banking net such interventions cannot be as successful as they are intended to be (Mehrotra and Yetman 2014).

2.2 Importance of FI: Empirical Studies

Empirical studies have shown that financial inclusion is both pro-poor as well as pro-growth. It provides benefits to the households as well as small and microenterprises in the country, and facilitates economic transactions for a large number of new economic agents. Financial inclusion helps low income families to access financial services like savings, credit, insurance etc. These financial services can be used to gain access to education, health care and other necessities to improve their quality of life. With access to financial services, small and microenterprises get an opportunity to use their savings and credit to make productive investments. This in turn fosters financial independence and thus enhances economic growth. (Sarath Chandra and Manju 2010).

Improved financial services not only enhance growth but also reduce poverty and income inequality (Beck et al. 2009). A cross country regression analysis suggests that countries having low GDP per capita, relatively higher levels of income inequality, low rates of literacy, low urbanisation and poor connectivity seem to be less financially inclusive (Sarma and Pias 2008).

Despite having such apparent advantages, innumerable practical issues come in the way of expansion and extension of financial services to a large population. In context to this, the following literature review is divided into a few major concerns associated with financial inclusion.

2.2.1 Infrastructure and Financial Inclusion

One of the major issues associated with financial inclusion is infrastructure. Availability of infrastructure both financial as well as physical should grow parallel to each other. Inefficient accessibility to credit sources weakens the financial status of the economy. Hence, to ensure access to the available credit sources, there is need to create equally efficient financial infrastructure. Studies show that, besides availability of infrastructural facilities and urbanisation of a state, greater availability of banking services can foster financial inclusion, particularly among the low income households (Pal and Pal 2012). Availability of financial infrastructure can help asset recognition by the poor from financial investments (Sarath Chandra and Manju 2010). But in terms of financial infrastructure, there are lacunas with the banking sector such as lack of national and commercial bank branches in rural areas, inaccessibility to ATM's etc., and hence the need to set up more financial institutions like banks, credit bureau, property registries, etc. In order to ease the access to financial sources, Raghuram Rajan Committee made recommendations and suggestions like introducing unique national ID number with biometric information, providing existing subsidies and cash transfers to the poor via banks etc. to encourage use of banking infrastructure by the people.

But the existence of financial infrastructure wouldn't be advantageous if there is no accessibility to it. Therefore to access the available facilities, there should also be a well-established physical infrastructure connecting people to the financial services.

Empirical studies suggest that Physical infrastructure like the network of paved roads, telephone, internet subscription etc. is highly positively significant for enhancing financial inclusion (Sarma and Pais 2008). Chattopadhyay (2011) in his study has cited how improvement in infrastructure in rural West Bengal in terms of electricity, roads, telecommunications, etc. would establish a better overall supply chain management and enhance productivity of physical resources in the rural areas, and lead to greater demand for banking services among the rural population. But infrastructure connecting to banking services is very scarce in nature in many less developed nations. Demirgüç-Kunt and Klapper (2012) in their study in Kenya have found that poor infrastructure and telecommunications and heavy branch regulation, have indeed restricted the geographical expansion of bank branches in that country. Also in India, poor infrastructure has led to poor market linkage which in turn has caused inaccessibility to financial services in poor states like Madhya Pradesh (Rather and Lone 2012).

2.2.2 Innovations and Financial Inclusion

The lack of access to adequate physical infrastructure can be compensated by innovations in banking.

In this context technological innovations are important as technology not only enhances the competitive efficiency of the banking sector by strengthening back-end administrative processes; it also improves the front-end operations and helps in bringing down the transaction costs for the customers. Information and communication, technology (ICT) solutions continue to help banks in providing seamless systems to capture customer data, ensure unique identification, and facilitate financial transaction services using remote connectivity. These systems also ensure uninterrupted service delivery, consumer data protection, customized products, dissemination of information on credit operations, and offer multiple financial products in local languages (Prabha et al. 2013). Use of technology such as payment cards or mobile phones helps easy identification of customers and record transactions electronically and also enables customers to initiate transactions remotely through third party outlets such as post offices and small retailers as agents (Handoo 2010). Technology has the potential of furthering financial inclusion by making small ticket retail transactions cheaper, easier and faster for the banking sector as well as for the small customers (Gupta 2011; Thorat 2008). Innovations such as mobile banking have reduced the cost of transaction and have made payments electronically transferrable and cheaper (Raghuram Rajan Committe Report 2008; Ismail and Masinge 2012).

Using econometric analysis Ismail and Masinge (2012) have identified some of the factors that have influenced introduction of mobile banking by Banks in South Africa, such as perceived usefulness, perceived ease-of use, perceived cost, and the level of customer trust in mobile banking. A major technological development in banking sector is the adoption of core banking solutions which entails networking of branches, enable customers to operate their bank account and avail services regardless of the location, while the advent of ATM's, e-payments, NEFT etc. seamlessly connects people to financial services (Gupta 2011). Another approach is of "banks on wheels" in which a vehicle-mounted bank counter visits areas without regular bank-branches at regular intervals to enable people to make transaction. This model has been found successful in Kenya (Dupas et al. 2012).

Besides technological innovations, the introduction of Business correspondent model and Agency banking by RBI have also revolutionised banking sector in India (Thorat 2010). Bank-led and technology driven Business Correspondent (BC) model was launched in 2006 in India for expansion of branchless banking and to bring about financial inclusion. Handheld models like Business correspondent (BC)/business facilitator model (BF) formulated by RBI have helped to strengthen financial access by extending banking network to far-flung off rural areas in order to provide door to door service to the local populace (Sarath Chandra and Manju 2010). Banks should be enabled to tie up with non-banks through appropriate agency arrangements in order to equip/empower pharmacies, post-offices and super markets not only as agents of banks but also as agents of financial inclusion.

On the lines of the roles and responsibilities of business correspondents (BC's) the contracted entities can undertake the preliminary work relating to account opening formalities, but responsibility for ensuring compliance with know your customer (KYC) norms should remain with the banks. BCs should also aim to create awareness about savings and other products and provide education and advice on managing money and perform debt counselling (Oxford Policy Management Ltd 2011).

Though the BC model was implemented to enhance financial inclusion, there are various unresolved issues associated with it. Prabha et al. (2013) in their study have stated that the BC system lack commercial viability and also adversely affect the Customer service point (CSP) employed by the BC. The other problems associated with it were the selection of BC through bidding system, lack of financial literacy program, operational risk, poor banking knowledge etc. In contrast to the problems associated with BC models, Prabha et al. (2013) make certain recommendations, which include provision for a thorough review of business correspondents by RBI or Indian bank federation before selecting them, promoting viability gap funding to increase investments promoting financial literacy, rewarding BCs who perform better by authorising more products like small loans, etc. and to develop alternate channels like ATM's, internet banking etc. The remuneration structure of BC's has been very flexible since its implementation. From 2006 to 2009 the BC's were not allowed to charge anything to the consumers, but this restriction was removed in 2009 to encourage uptake of BC model; since then banks and BC's have been charging a reasonable sums from customers as service charge (Oxford Policy Management 2011).

A cross country analysis suggests that agents have been found to offer cheaper (Peru in particular), more accessible (Brazil in particular), and appropriate financial products (Kenya in particular). Therefore, agents can be a key tool for enabling more and more people to open bank accounts, particularly where they have been used to receive CCT payments. Agent networks can also be instrumental in providing important feed-backs to their Banks about their customers. (Oxford Policy Management Ltd 2011).

2.2.3 Financial Literacy and Financial Inclusion

Innovations alone cannot solve the problem of financial inclusion. To utilise the services provided by the banks, it is important that the individuals have the knowledge and skill to use those services. Therefore, financial literacy is one of the very important aspects in promoting financial inclusion. Without financial literacy, and the knowledge to use financial services provided, the financial infrastructure put in place would remain under- used, and therefore result in huge wastage of scarce resources. Hence, financial literacy and customer education has to run parallel to the programmes like Business correspondent models (Prabha et al. 2013). One of the studies by Diaz and Zekri (2013) on Bhutanese population shows that in spite of having a long term saving goal, most of the respondents couldn't reach it due to poor financial management skills and therefore remedial steps had to be recommended to increase the management skills that would improve the ability to access formal financial services.

Collard et al. (2001) reported widespread lack of knowledge about financial products and services and basic money management skills as the issues related to financial literacy in Bristol, and recommended initiation of school based schemes which provide money management skills and financial education as the remedial measure. Other suggestions they provided include independent advice and explanation on financial instruments by an individual who understands finance, face-to-face programmes for adults etc.

Though a number of studies highlight existence of financial illiteracy among rural population, there are also evidences which show that financial illiteracy among large segments of urban population has limited their access to financial services (Sarath Chandra and Manju 2010). Considering these problems arising out of financial illiteracy, the Rajan committee (Rajan 2008) emphasises the need of providing financial literacy from early schooling years by introducing children to financial terms such as income, expenditure, savings, deposits etc. In addition, TV channels could also be encouraged to run educational programmes on household budgeting etc.

In context to the importance of financial literacy, Rai and Saha (2010) have not only emphasised the importance of financial literacy on the demand end, but also on the supply end where proper training should be provided to bank staff and the field staff to communicate with the customers. Also emphasised is the need to eliminate financial illiteracy at the demand-side by educating the masses of the availability of new banking products like No-frill accounts, etc. and the flexibility of the system to suit the specific needs of the customer. With an aim to spread financial literacy, RBI has formulated a Model scheme for Financial Literacy and Credit Counselling Centres (FLCCCs) and advised Lead Banks to open a Financial Literacy and Credit Counselling Centre (FLCCC) in conformity with the Model Scheme in every district where they have lead responsibility. The objectives of this scheme have been to educate rural and urban population about financial products, to provide face to face financial counselling, to formulate debt restructuring etc. (RBI 2010).

Thus we observe from the review that literature on financial inclusion is either general in nature or rural centric and that there is a lack of studies that focus on urban exclusion, the nature of which is quite different from its rural counterpart. This study is meant chiefly to fill this gap, using both secondary and field level primary data. However, before going to the Indian experiences it is useful to get a global perspective of the problem of financial exclusion and measures taken by different countries to address the problems. Some of these measures we present in the following Chapter; they need not necessarily be for urban populace alone, but nonetheless provide valuable information regarding endeavours of different countries especially developing and emerging nations in this regard.

References

Banerjee A, Newman A (1993) Occupational choice and the process of development. J Polit Econ 101(2):274–298
Beck T, Demirgüç-Kunt A, Honohan P (2009) Access to financial services: measurement, impact, and policies. World Bank Research Paper 24(1) World Bank, Washington, D.C
Chattopadhyay SK (2011) Financial inclusion in India: a case of West Bengal, RBI working paper series
Collard S, Kempson E, Whyley C (2001) Tackling financial exclusion. Policy press, Bristol
Demirgüç-Kunt A, Klapper F (2012) Measuring financial inclusion: The global findex database. World bank policy research working paper no. 6025
Diamond DW, Dybvig P (1983) Bank runs. Deposit Insur Liquidity J Polit Econ 91:401–419
Diaz KS, Zekri S (2013) Appendix D. Technical note on focus group survey in bhutan
Dupas P, Green S, Keats A, Robinson J (2012) Challenges in banking the rural poor: Evidence from kenya's western province (No. w17851). National Bureau of Economic Research.
Galor O, Zeira J (1993) Income distribution and macroeconomics. Rev Econ Stud 60(1):35–52
Gupta A (2011) Towards financial inclusion in india. SAMVAD, SIBM Pune, 68
Handoo J (2010) Financial inclusion in India: Integration of technology, policy and market at the bottom of the pyramid. Available at SSRN: https://ssrn.com/abstract=1628564
Harrison P et al (1999): Finance and growth: theory and new evidence, Federal Reserve Board Discussion paper no. 35, July
Ismail T, Masinge K (2012) Mobile banking: innovation for the poor. African journal of science, technology, innovation and development, 4(3), 98–127
Mehrotra A, Yetman J (2014) Financial Inclusion and Optimal Monetary Policy, Bank of International Settlements Working paper no. 476, BIS
Oxford Policy Management Ltd (2011) Enhancing Financial innovation & Access, "Evaluation of Agent Banking Models in different countries". www.efina.org.ng
Pal R, Pal R (2012) Income related inequality in financial inclusion and role of banks: evidence on financial exclusion in India, IGIDR Working paper no. 2012–13
Prabha R, Dayal S, Bhist HS (2013) A study on the efficacy of business correspondent model, The Association of community development finance institutions, Citi group
Rai A, Saha A (2010) Financial inclusion in karnataka: a study of operationalisation of no frills accounts, MPRA paper no. 26528
Rajan Raghuram G (2008) A hundred small steps-report of the committee on financial sector reforms. Planning Commission, Government of India, pp 64–87
Rajeev Meenakshi B, Vani P. (2011) Farm sector in karnataka: Farmers' indebtedness and risk management, project No. CESP/93, Institute for social and economic change, Bengaluru
Rather NA, Lone PA. (2012) Bottlenecks and problems related to financial inclusion in madhya pradesh. J Econ Sustain Dev 3(9):11–20
RBI (2010) RBI bulletin, RBI, Mumbai
Romer Paul M (1986) Increasing returns and long run growth. J Polit Econ 94(5):1002–1037
Romer Paul M (1990) Endogenous technological change. J Polit Econ 98(5):S71–S102
Sarath Chandra BP, Manju TK (2010) Financial inclusion strategies for inclusive growth in India, MPRA paper, no. 33569
Sarma M, Pais J (2008) Financial inclusion and development-A cross country analysis, ICRIER Working paper, August 2008
Schumpeter JA (1934) The theory of economic development, Leipzig: Dunker and Humbolt, 1912; translated by Redvers Opie, Cambridge, MA, Harvard University Press
Subbarao D (2013) Financial literacy and financial inclusion are integral to each other, speeches at the India-OECD-World Bank Regional Conference Bis Speeches. www.bis.org/review
Thiel M (2001) Finance and economic growth-a review of theory and the available evidence (No. 158). Directorate General Economic and Financial Affairs (DG ECFIN), European Commission
Thorat U (2008) Financial inclusion and information technology. Speech published in RBI bulletin, October 2008
Thorat U (2010) Financial regulator and financial inclusion-working at cross purposes, BIS Review, 77

Chapter 3
Financial Exclusion of the Poor: Global Experiences

Before moving on to the Indian case it is of interest to highlight the problems of financial exclusion in general for other countries across the globe and the innovative endeavours of some of the less developed and emerging nations to include the under privileged under the banking net. In this context it is worth noting that there is an increasing concern, especially in the less developed and emerging nations, regarding the level of financial inclusion of the poor. Majority of the world's adult population, mostly above the age of 18 do not have access to financial services in the formal sector despite being conscious of the benefits of bank access (Beck et al. 2007). They are seriously handicapped in their day-today struggle for sustenance and upward mobility for want of access to formal banking. A majority of this population, known as the 'under-banked' or 'unbanked' is disproportionately concentrated in the developing countries of South Asia, Africa and the Middle East and North Africa (MENA) region (Demirguc-Kunt et al. 2015). In recognition of the immense benefits for the individual in particular and the nation in general, a concerted effort is being made to bring more people into the fold of formal financial system around the world at all levels. In terms of implementation, the progress achieved is also commendable. In fact 700 million adults across the world became new holders of accounts between 2011 and 2014, a massive 20% increase since 2010 (Demirguc-Kunt et al 2015). According to data collected across countries by the UN Secretary-General's Special Advocate for Inclusive Finance for Development, this commendable success comes after years of banking sector reforms made across these countries (UNSGSA Report 2014).

To understand the magnitude of the problem, the respective countries as well as the international organisations are showing interest in measuring the level of exclusion. Interesting case studies of countries across the globe are also getting reviewed. The World Bank has recently allowed access to a global data set (viz., Findex) that measures financial exclusion in 148 countries covering a large number of indicators relating to access and usage of financial intermediaries.

This chapter has benefitted greatly from the assistance we received from Supriya Bhandarkar, Pranav Nagendran and Anu Jose. We thank them immensely for their help.

M. Rajeev and B.P. Vani, *Financial Access of the Urban Poor in India*,
SpringerBriefs in Economics, DOI 10.1007/978-81-322-3712-9_3

The report highlights (see http://www.worldbank.org/en/topic/financialinclusion/overview#1 for more details) that about 2 billion people (estimated to be 38% of adults in the world) appear to have no accessibility to formal financial institutions. Needless to say, the poor are particularly deprived and as high as 73% of the poor are financially excluded. Among other factors, income is one of the prime determinants of accessibility and data from World Bank reveals that income wise the top 20% of adults population from developing nations are more than twice likely to own an account in any formal financial institution compared to the bottom 20% people of the country. In the developing countries, the poor are largely self employed and in regular need of funds for productive purposes. Therefore, they are in much greater need to have access to better financial services, absence of which may force them to borrow from money lenders under adverse terms and conditions.

We present a few selected indicators for different countries in this chapter (see Tables 3.1 and 3.2). As is evident from the tables, the inequality between the high income and low income countries is striking. For example, in 2014, 53% people in India have bank accounts against 99% in Germany.

Notably, much of the effort in terms of enabling the masses to get access to financial services has taken place at individual country levels, where the government along with private and public financial institutions have successfully rolled out policies and programmes to make access easier for all. Several models have been tried across the world and innovations in terms of cheaper and faster solutions such as electronic payments have enabled financial services to reach even the remotest of areas. Experiences worldwide have, however, proved that there is no single solution to the problem of financial exclusion and the various models used have had different degrees of success in different countries of the world (Bansal 2012). One common feature that stands out across regions has been the rise of not traditional forms of banking but alternative forms of financial services—such as mobile banking and non-banking channels largely complemented by the fact that developing economies are characterized by increasing use of mobile services, improvements in technology and large scale innovation which have cut costs in terms of money and time (Huefner 2015).

In the following section, international experiences in terms of different financial services including account ownership, savings, borrowings, insurance, money transfers and payments used by individuals and firms are described. In addition, taking into account the broadening financial landscape, experiences of countries providing financial education are also relied upon. We first consider innovations and practices undertaken to increase account ownership. For most people, having a formal account is the first step towards financial inclusion. Having a formal account enables transfer of wages or remittances and may encourage savings and enhance access to credit. Practices to mobilize savings and encourage access to credit and insurance from formal institutions are also separately considered. Finally programmes to improve financial literacy across the globe are highlighted.

The discussions below highlight the progress taking place in selected countries only. However innovations in terms of financial inclusion are taking place across

Table 3.1 Global Financial Index, 2011: Country and income wise distribution

	Lower middle income			Low income		Middle income			High income: OECD		
	India	Bangladesh	Total: lower middle	Nepal	Total: low	Brazil	Mexico	Total: middle income	Germany	USA	Total: high income OECD
Account	35.2	31.7	28.6	25.3	21.1	55.8	27.4	43.3	98.1	87.9	89.9
ATMs (per 100,000 adults)	8.8	3.6	13.1	7.4	2.1	117.8	43.7	27.9	118.7	NA	96.0
Credit card	1.7	0.9	2.1	0.6	1.8	29.2	12.9	7.0	35.7	61.9	50.7
Debit card	8.3	2.2	10.0	3.7	6.3	41.1	22.2	24.5	88	71.7	61.9
Account, female	26.4	26	23.0	21.2	17.5	51.1	21.9	38.3	98.7	84	88.3
Formal credit	7.6	23.3	7.3	10.8	11.7	6.3	7.5	7.6	12.5	20.1	14.1
Purchased agricultural insurance	6.6	0	4.6	2.2	6.0	NA	NA	6.2	NA	NA	NA
Received domestic remittances	NA[a]	NA	NA	NA	NA	NA	NA	NA	NA	NA	NA
Savings	11.6	16.6	13.6	9.9	13.2	10.28	6.7	19.8	55.9	50.3	47.2
Account, income, poorest 40%	27.3	21.2	20.0	14.4	12.5	39.4	11.9	30.7	98.7	80.9	87.7

Global Financial Index, 2011: Country and income wise distribution

Note 1. [a]Data not available

2. All figures are (age 15+, %)

Source World Bank

Table 3.2 Global Financial Index, 2014: Country and income wise distribution

	Lower middle income			Low income		Middle income			High income: OECD		
	India	Bangladesh	Total: lower middle	Nepal	Total: low	Brazil	Mexico	Total: middle income	Germany	USA	Total: high income OECD
Account	53.1	30.9	42.7	33.8	27.5	68.1	39.1	57.5	98.7	93.5	94.0
ATMs (per 100,000 adults)	NA	NA	NA	NA	NA	NA	NA	NA	NA	NA	NA
Credit card	4.17	0.3	3.7	0.4	1.0	32	17.8	10.7	45.8	60.1	52.9
Debit card	22	5.1	21.1	6.7	6.5	59.1	26.8	34.4	91.9	76.2	79.6
Account, female	42.6	25.2	35.4	31.3	19.2	64.7	38.8	52.5	99.4	94.7	93.7
Formal credit	6.3	9.8	7.5	11.9	8.5	11.9	10.4	9.0	18.6	23.2	18.3
Purchased agricultural insurance	NA[a]	NA	NA	NA	NA	NA	NA	NA	NA	NA	NA
Received domestic remittances	9.7	14.1	17.8	24.1	25.5	6.4	11.6	17.8	NA	NA	NA
Savings	14.3	7.4	17.5	16.4	11.3	12.3	14.4	25.9	57.9	54.1	52.8
Account, income, poorest 40%	43.7	21.5	32.3	23.7	14.8	58.4	28.5	48.6	97	87.1	90.5

Note 1. [a]Data not available
2. All figures are (age 15+, %)
Source World Bank

the globe on a large scale, thereby enabling financial security as a policy priority in many countries.

It is, however, important to note that several low and middle income countries today are using various innovative models to enhance financial access of the poor, and a few such cases are worth discussing. At the end of this chapter we present three selected case studies from countries across the globe.

3.1 Key Indicators of Financial Inclusion

3.1.1 Account Ownership

Holding a bank account is one of the most important indicators of being included in the formal financial system since all formal financial activity in today's world takes place through banks and bank accounts (World Bank 2014). The Global Findex database states that since 2011, 700 million people across the globe have become first time account holders, and that the number of people who did not have an account dropped by 20% to 2 billion by 2014. Extent to which population of a country own formal bank accounts varies significantly across the globe. For low income, developing economies on an average around 54% of citizens have access to formal financial services which the corresponding figure for developed OECD countries is as high as 94% (Fig. 3.1). Within the less developed nations there is wide variations too. For example, in East Asia and Pacific around 70% of people have access to accounts in the formal banking sector but for Middle East account penetration figure can be as low as 14%, depicting wide ranging disparity across the developing countries.

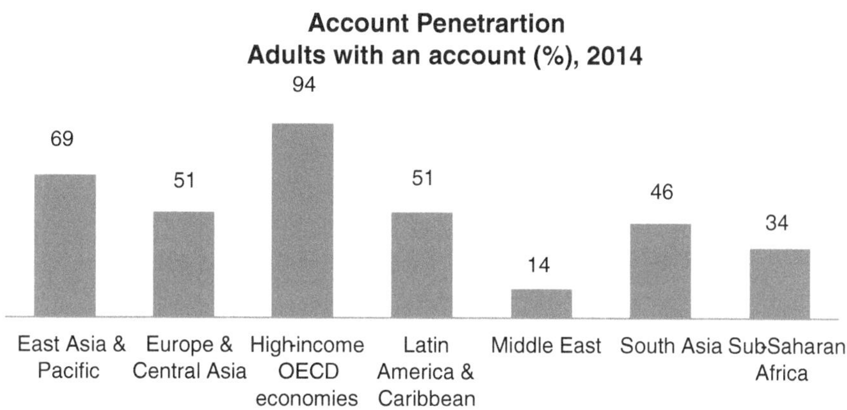

Fig. 3.1 Share of adults with an account (in percentages), 2014 *Source* Compiled using global Findex database

Majority of the adults across the globe attribute not having a formal bank account due to the high costs of banking services such as the monthly maintenance fees charged in most African countries that can be as high as $4 per month (Triki and Faye 2013), fees charged for opening a bank account and also the minimum balance requirements that cannot be met in most countries. In addition, there are various indirect costs such as time taken to travel to the bank and the complicated documentation requirement that act as a deterrent to either opening or using an account.

In order to bring about more people into the fold of the formal banking system, governments of various countries across the world have introduced innovative measures and expanded the regulatory framework making it easier and more conducive to own accounts. Some such innovations involve opening of basic accounts, use of banking correspondent or agents representing particular banks, use of mobile technology to ensure easy accessibility, low deposit requirement or reducing procedural complications and so on which are highlighted below.

3.1.1.1 Basic Accounts

In order to overcome the problem of high costs, which make small transactions a burden for significant parts of the population, various countries are offering innovative and cost effective financial services such as basic accounts that demand only low level of balance, free transactions per month and other technology based services.

The Central Bank of Brazil[1] introduced simplified bank accounts in the year 2000 in order to eliminate the barriers that kept approximately 80% of its population outside the framework of formal financial services. Banks were directed to open accounts based on identity proof with no income or address proof demanded. A positive balance maintained in these accounts for up to 90 days, made the account holder eligible for a loan up to R$200 (US$117) which if further extended to 180 days, could mean that credit up to R$600 could be availed—without any additional information except identity card numbers. An estimated 8.75 million such accounts also known as CaixaFácil accounts were opened within a span of 10 years.

In South Africa,[2] considered one of the costlier banking markets in the world, the central bank directed five banks to launch a 'no-frill' bank account scheme. In 2004, the Mzansi scheme was launched which allowed negligible minimum deposits, no monthly fees and allowed five free transactions per month. The

[1]Brazil: Mettenheim (2013) New perspectives on banking and agendas for financial inclusion (Doctoral dissertation, Harvard Kennedy School, Cambridge Massachusetts).

[2]South Africa: Triki and Faye (2013) Financial Inclusion in Africa. Tunisia: African Development Bank.

collaboration between the banks allowed these account holders to withdraw money from any banks ATM at no extra charges. Due to this scheme, there were 6 million mzansi accounts opened in a country of 32 million people by the year 2009, with a large section of the informal sector being brought into the formal banking sector coverage.

However, by August 2008 approximately 30% of these mzansi accounts were inactive or closed. Further, the level of usage, the average balances and the fee income generated were 55, 85 and 70 percentages lower than commercial banks respectively, while the cash withdrawal rate was 16% higher as compared to commercial banks in the country. Due to the above factors, the banks began to realise that these accounts were unviable for them in terms of profits and hence stopped marketing them even though they were still available (Forbes India 2011).

In the United States, the State of New York Banking Department passed the Banking Law with the objective of making available the low cost banking services to consumers. This banking law made it mandatory that each bank shall offer a basic banking account and each credit union a basic share draft account, which shall be low cost with minimum facilities. This enabled a customer to open a bank account with a maximum deposit of US$25 where the minimum balance required was only US$0.10. There were additional advantages such as no charges for withdrawals up to eight times during a periodic cycle, and the charges for the maintenance of such accounts were to be declared up front. Along the same lines, in Indonesia,[3] Bank Rakyat Indonesia (BRI) introduced a basic account to eradicate financial exclusion. This type of accounts are free from any kind of charges up to four transactions per month and required a minimum deposit of Rp 5,000 ($0.53). Deposits as low as those above Rp 10,000 ($1.06) also earned interest.

In Europe,[4] over 57 million citizens do not have bank accounts especially in regions of Bulgaria and Romania. In order to rectify this lacuna the EU Parliament in 2015 passed an order that mandated all financial institutions in Europe to guarantee all citizens, including migrants the capability to open basic bank accounts. These bank accounts were to have fees that would be charged in a straightforward manner. In order to ensure that this was carried out, all member-states were also required to create websites that gave information regarding the tariffs relating to these accounts.

While basic bank accounts have undoubtedly increased the percentage of population having access to financial services, ownership of these accounts does not always translate into benefits. Most of these accounts lie dormant due to factors such as the long travel time to reach a bank branch. For example, in Tanzania where

[3]Robinson (2004) "Why the Bank Rakyat Indonesia Has the World's Largest Sustainable Microbanking System." In *BRI* International Seminar, Bali, Indonesia.

[4]European Commission (2011) "Commission Recommendation on Access to a Basic Payment Account." European Commission, Brussels.

as large as 47% of the population are unbanked and people cited distance as a key factor for their not opening/holding an account (Demirgüç-Kunt and Klapper 2013).

In order to address this issue, countries have gone beyond opening traditional bank branches and brought about innovations such as teaming up with retail outlets, hiring bank agents, opening up rural branches etc., that do not require the customers to travel long distances wasting both time and money, thereby remedying the above constraint.

3.1.1.2 Branchless Banking

Branchless banking, often defined as a way to deliver financial services without relying on bank branches has spread rapidly in most markets. This is also a boon in areas where opening a branch is not feasible in terms of high risks involved or other reasons such as lack of security in remote areas. Branchless banking has now emerged as an innovative method to reduce financial exclusion in such regions. Channels such as mobile or internet banking, bank agents etc. attempt to solve these logistical problems (CGAP 2009). Various forms of branchless banking are highlighted below.

3.1.1.3 Bank Agents[5]

Banking Agents serve as 'doorstep bankers' and provide the much needed last mile connectivity to reach out to the millions of customers in the rural areas across the globe where opening a brick and mortar branch is not feasible. This helps banks provide services to people at their homes through the use of third party services.

Brazil increased the number of account holders from 39% in 2011 to 51% in 2014 by being one of the first countries to adopt a branchless banking framework in the 1970s by popularising financial services among the masses through agents. Noteworthily, Brazil created a network of around 150,000 banking agents, alternatively known as "banking correspondents," who worked towards ensuring banking facility for the poor. As a result of such wide spread network, as high as 2.6 billion transactions were made in the country; in particular, by the year 2011, all of the 5564 municipalities of the country were covered by at least one bank branch, or by banking agents where it is reported that quarter of these are served only by correspondents, showing the strength of the network.

Banking agents are used for facilitating financial inclusion in Ecuador as well where banks such as Banco de Guayaquil are known for having a strong network of correspondents. They have been able to create a network of more than 3,600 banking correspondents; one of the prime responsibilities of these agents is to make popular a simplified account known as "cuentaamiga," as a kit which among

[5]Triki and Faye (2013) Financial Inclusion in Africa. Tunisia: African Development Bank.

others consists of an activated debit card and a user manual. Documentation requirement for activating an account given through the kit has also made minimal and thereby a quick process is ensured. Given such initiatives as high as 250,000 accounts were opened in a span of about 1 year. Given the advantage of Banking correspondent model, financial intermediaries from other nations such as Banco Estado in Chile, Bancolombia in Colombia and Ban rural in Guatemala are also using such correspondent to reach the hitherto unbanked population.

3.1.1.4 Correspondent Banking[6]

Correspondent Banking, wherein a retail outlet serves as an agent for a bank has become popular over the years. These retail outlets are often present at accessible locations and serve as a medium for customers to perform traditional banking activities such as deposits and withdrawal of cash, balance enquires and transfer of money across accounts.

Organizations in Latin America have started using post offices, grocery stores, and even kirana stores as agents. Since these outlets are widely used by the local population and are well known, the partnership between banks and these outlets are beneficial. The Mexican government too is planning to make use of its large network of Diconsa stores. These stores are managed by the local communities, sponsored by the government which sell food and agricultural supplies to the lower sections of the society. Due to its wide reach, these stores will be initially used to provide people with government transfers after which opening of accounts and other features such as insurance will be provided. This pilot programme has already reached nearly 200,000 households.

3.1.1.5 Non Business Correspondent Based Model: Use of Technology for Branchless Banking

Innovative Business Models in an attempt to provide round the clock financial services with minimum paperwork, easy access and low transaction costs have introduced various forms of mobile and internet banking.

3.1.1.6 Mobile Banking[7]

In most countries where infrastructure is poor but have increasing mobile network coverage, the concept of mobile money—often called M-money, increasingly

[6]See Global Financial Inclusion: Achieving full financial inclusion at the intersection of social benefit and economic sustainability. McKinsey & Company.

[7]Donovan (2012) Mobile money for financial inclusion. Information and communication for development, 61–73.

becoming popular. This mobile money can be bought, and kept in their account and can be used to make various purchases.

Safaricom, a mobile network that is a subsidiary of the Vodafone group, the largest in Kenya, first started this through a programme called M-Pesa. Mobile money can be used by customers for purchases, to transfer money to a third party, pay off loans or could even be exchanged for cash at one of the ATMs or outlets across Kenya. A minimal fixed transaction fee was charged for these services. The amount of money spent could be immediately tracked on a real time basis and therefore help one keep a track of financial management. Given these advantages 70% of households in Kenya adopted this facility (Kendall 2010; Mas and Radcliffe 2011). This, mostly cashless method of banking, has also been useful in a country where there were a large number of cash based thefts.

The South African Bank of Athens too launched a mobile banking network known as WIZZIT that had the same features of M-Pesa. Transaction fees charged for these accounts were less than a third of that charged by commercial banks. South African Bank also recruited people known as WIZZ kids and trained them in the usage and advantages of these accounts. These WIZZ kids would explain the same to potential customers and could earn commission if anyone signed up. This model was so successful that WIZZIT is now the largest branch network in South Africa.

Since then, several other countries have introduced mobile banking systems such as Easypaisa in Pakistan, bKash in Bangladesh, Smart in Philippines and M-Paisa in Afghanistan increasing the popularity and proliferation of mobile money services.

3.1.1.7 Electronic Government Payments

Electronic government payments, wherein the government directly credits the money into the payee's bank account too have contributed to financial inclusion. For instance, Brazil's Bolsa Familia system, a social welfare programme covers 12.4 million beneficiaries who have children in order to enable them to send children to school and get them vaccinated. Prospera, a welfare programme founded in Mexico in 2002, too relies on government electronic payments to ensure that beneficiaries receive funds for education and health expenses. These electronic payments by governments in formal financial institutions in turn ensured financial inclusion of the poor beneficiaries (World Bank 2012b).

3.1.1.8 Point of Transaction Machines

An alternate way to provide banking services in the remote areas where brick and mortar branches are difficult to ensure is by making available point of transaction (POT) machines. This facility provides more number of services than an ATMs by giving the user an opportunity to transact in different accounts; more importantly to debit and credit money to other accounts. An example from Nepal is worth mentioning here. This programme initiated in 2013 and named as 'Ghar Angan Banking Sewa', used POT machines to ensure banking facility for the poorer section especially living in remote regions (Aggarwal and Klapper 2013) Low balance account to the tune of only Nepal currency NPR 100 were made available together with cheque book facility, mobile and internet banking etc.

The ownership of accounts does not always translate to benefits. While the access to savings accounts has had a major impact on the amount saved, it is also seen that many accounts lie dormant with no deposits or withdrawals being made. In order to encourage savings and mobilize deposits, countries have started programmes that address the specific needs and constraints of poor households.

3.1.2 Savings

Savings to cover future expenses—education of children, weddings, illness, old age and purchases----is a universal practice. The extent of savings in formal financial institututions is also an important indicator of financial inclusion. However, the propensity and method of savings differs widely across and within regions. As seen below, in high income OECD countries 52% of the population saved at a financial institution while in the Middle East only a measly 4% reported as having done so (Fig. 3.2). Some of those people who have a formal account and still save using informal methods, such as keeping liquid cash at home are classified as 'underbanked'. These individuals choose such methods because the costs of using their account are prohibitively high and not conducive to saving. Due to this, banks today have come up with a variety of schemes to not only encourage opening of accounts but also to induce savings through formal institutions.

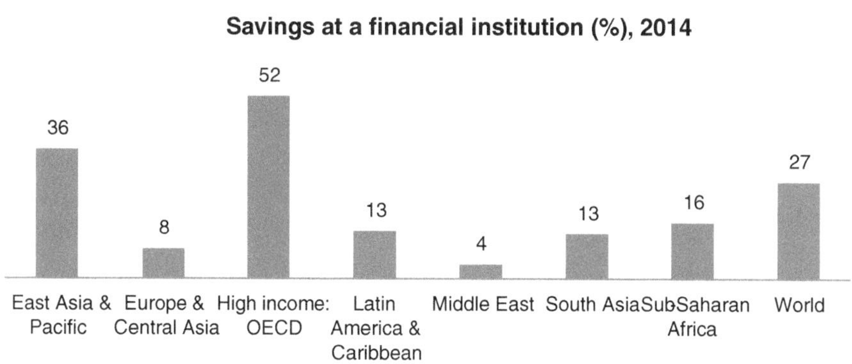

Fig. 3.2 Savings at a financial institution (% of people), 2014 *Source* Compiled using Global Findex Database (Demiguc-Kunt et al 2015)

In Bangladesh[8] where children above the age of 14 are allowed to work in non hazardous jobs, Bangladesh Bank pioneered a scheme wherein it introduced a service that allows children to open a savings account with participating banks for as little as 10 Taka without needing the co-signature of a parent or guardian, which is generally not possible for those children who are orphans or who have left home. These savings are managed by local NGOs approved by banks on behalf of the children up until they turn 18, after which they have full control and ownership of the accounts.

While many programmes have focussed their attention on efforts to decrease the monetary requirements to open a savings account, others have focused theirs towards ensuring that time and splurge consumption do not affect savings. Unlike regular savings accounts which allow money to be withdrawn at all times, commitment savings accounts offered by banks in Kenya and Philippines restrict the savers access to the funds up until a particular period of time or alternately up until a set target of savings has been reached (Goldberg 2014). This is found to have effectively increased the savings rate. In order to further enhance its feasibility, these accounts are often associated with labels and reminders.

In Kenya, citizens are encouraged to open a savings account for a specific purpose. They are then sent text messages mentioning the savings goals and reminding them to deposit the required money at regular intervals. Such initiatives are taken to remind the borrowers in case of Bolivia as well due to which savings increased by 6% on an average in banks. Messages also to increase the average amount deposited in the bank by helping savers keep sight of their goals and not withdraw money for any purpose other than for which it was originally designated.

In Indonesia,[9] BRI, the country's largest bank started a savings programme known as 'SimpananPedesaan' for citizens who owned small businesses in rural areas. These savings could be withdrawn at any time and savers could also take part in a lottery contest that the bank conducted from time to time. In UK the concept of 'Savings Gateway' was introduced by the Financial Inclusion Task Force. Under this scheme, those who have incomes below a certain set level, were encouraged to save with the state contributing 1£ for every 1£ the individual saved up to a maximum of £25 per month.

Rapid changes in technology too have promoted various innovative ways of savings such as Safaricom's M-Shwari accounts and Khushaal Munafa in Pakistan.

3.1.3 Borrowing

Another important indicator of financial inclusion is borrowing. If we look at the global figure, one finds that as far as adult population is concerned, 42% reported

[8]Judah (2013) Making Time: Helping child workers save their earnings. BBC News Magazine.

[9]Johnston and Morduch (2008) The unbanked: evidence from Indonesia. The World Bank Economic Review, 22(3), 517–537.

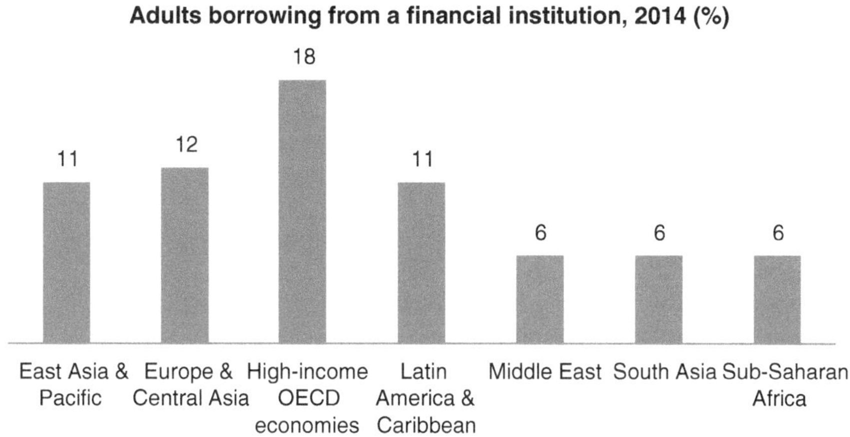

Fig. 3.3 Percentage of adults who borrowed from a financial institution (i.e., from a formal source), 2014 *Source* Compiled using Global Findex Database (Demiguc-Kunt et al 2015)

that they have borrowed funds (from both formal and informal sources) during the past 12 months. Though across region variations exist they were not substantial—Latin America and the Caribbean with 33%, and Sub-Saharan Africa at the top with 54%. But the sources of new loans varied widely among these regions (Demirguc-Kunt et al 2015).

As seen in the graph above(Fig. 3.3), borrowing from formal sources is quite low. Also, there was a wide variation among countries, mostly high income OECD countries—where 18% of adults borrowed from a financial institution—as against developing countries in the Middle East, South Asia and Sub Saharan Africa, where only 6% borrowed from a financial institution. Common reasons for taking a loan or borrowing money was to buy a house or invest in land, followed by having to pay for exorbitant medical bills, education and starting business.

In Indonesia, a major innovation was the general rural credit programme known as 'KreditUmumPedesaan' (Kupedes), which provided for monthly installment payments and was open to all borrowers for any purpose including agricultural, business and consumer loans. Timely repayment of the loan enabled a 25% refund of the interest that had been paid. Borrowers could also avail of a larger loan amount the next time if the instalments of the preceding loan was paid on time. This incentive helped loans from turning non productive, with 95% of the borrowers repaying their loan on time.

In Nigeria, Access Bank solved the problem of lack of collateral for undertaking a loan by introducing 'woman- friendly' collateral options wherein women are allowed to pledge their jewellery or other household items of value for obtaining a loan. Through this option, the program has enabled 1300 women to avail loans and get trained in financial management skills. The success of this programme inspired banks in Rwanda and Gambia to follow the model.

Exim bank in Tanzania too has developed a 'women friendly' financial product with the help of the International Finance Corporation and the Gender Action Plan. This was done when it was noticed that over 40% of Tanzanian women owned small businesses but had access only to 5% of formal credit. With the help of a 5 million US dollar loan, the program trained EXIM bank staff to work with women, helped establish a Women Program Unit and provided financial literary training to women to access loans in order to open and expand their small scale business. Till date, this had benefitted over 214 women and made them financially independent (World Bank 2011).

Mexico's Bancobank with a view to provide financial inclusion to the low and middle income groups of the population, opened more than 800 branches, all at once, in stores selling consumer goods known as 'Grupo Elektra'. Taking advantage of the stores' vast consumer base the bank was able to open accounts for those who did not have access to formal financial services but often visited the store.

3.1.4 Insurance

In Kenya, the Sygenta Foundation for Sustainable Agriculture developed an insurance product called Kilimo Salama (Meaning 'Safe Farming' in Swahili) for Kenyan farmers that spread through mobile technology. An index-based insurance product, it helped farmers invest in their farms by covering the input of farmers in the event of drought or even excessive rainfall. This was the first indexed micro insurance product launched through a mobile network—Safari.com helping—by covering 12,000 farmers in 2012 and 187,000 farmers in 2013, most with land less than five hectares in remote areas. Today, this has become the largest agricultural insurance product in Kenya due to the fact that it does not rely on expensive farm visits but on automated weather stations and mobile payments, reducing administrative costs and enabling a large number of farmers to avail of insurance without the hefty premiums.

A similar indexed insurance program has been developed in Malawi by the World Bank in association with National Smallholder Farmers' Association of Malawi, the Opportunity Bank of Malawi, and the Malawi Rural Finance Company. These indexed insurance programs ensure payment when natural weather conditions deviated from the normal set standard. Since this could not be controlled by policy holders, there was no risk of moral hazard, just to get a claim of the money. In Morocco, AlAmana Microfinance, a women's world banking network member, introduced a micro insurance scheme called L'Assistance ('help' in French) which was provided when each client availed a loan. This insurance policy provided cash to women at times of financial need such as childbirth or for paying medical bills. Thanks to this novel scheme, around 240,000 previously uninsured women in the country have insurance today though the claims have been as low as 20% (Crepon et al. 2011).

3.2 Financial Literacy

Increasing financial inclusion around the world requires a combination of provision of financial services and increasing financial knowledge of customers in order to help them make informed decisions. This is particularly needed for women who are considered less financially literate than men, to increase their economic empowerment and financial inclusion. It is often also seen that even in regions where the financial markets are well developed, people are usually less informed in terms of financial knowledge (Lusardi and Mitchell 2011).

In fact, it is often noticed that financial knowledge in turn helps people use the available financial services in a more efficient manner due to which a large number of countries have been providing financial education to a wide group of people, often consciously focussing on inclusion of women and children (Atkinson and Messy 2013). A few nations, including India have perceived that there are risks in launching new financial products for customers without providing financial knowledge as uninformed customers are prone to making wrong financial decisions. A survey of financial regulators from 142 economies conducted in 2010 showed that 88% of nations have some aspect of financial education present in their policy (CGAP 2010).

Aflatoun, an NGO headquartered in the Netherlands, has started a program to make financial training accessible to school kids by creating educational modules that teach children about various aspects of money through games. It has also had some initial success in its campaign for inclusion of financial education in national school curriculum (e.g. in Egypt).

Indonesia has developed a National Strategy for Financial Education which was launched in June 2012. In Malaysia, Bank Negara considers financial inclusion as one its primary objectives. The bank states that 'financial literacy, advisory and awareness' are key to a strong financial sector that is all-encompassing and does so through the provision of help desks that provide financial knowledge such as debt counselling, investment options etc. to consumers. In the Philippines, the National Strategy for Financial Inclusion ensures that financial education is imparted in school in both urban and rural areas. Concepts of saving, budgeting, spending and the risks and returns of certain investments are taught through a specially designed curriculum by the Department of Education of Philippines.

Having discussed the major components of financial inclusion and the experiences of different nations across the globe, the study now proceeds to present a few interesting case studies.

3.3 Country Experiences: Three Case Studies

3.3.1 SACCO in Rwanda

After a Survey conducted by Finscope in 2008 brought to light that a mere 21% of Rwanda's population who were considered to be bankable were making use of formal financial services and fully financially excluded population were as high as 52%, the state perceived that it is the time for some action. The concept of Umurenge Savings and Credit Cooperatives (SACCOs) was introduced to enhance financial inclusion in different administrative sectors (called Umurenge). Savings and Credit Co-operative (SACCO) is a type of co-operative institution which aims at pooling savings from the members and in turn attempt to meet their credit needs. Thus the concept is somewhat similar to the concept of self help group or cooperative banks in India or Bangladesh. In addition, SACCOs are supposed to help the poor to understand proper management of funds and also how to make good investments. SACCOs were not limited to the rural areas where banking facilities are limited, urban population who were regular salaried or earned some wages also became part of Urban SACCOs; in the rural areas it is the farmer groups that primarily constituted SACCOs. But SACCO's are not limited to farmer members alone as people from other professions such as traders or transport operators or jua kalis also became part of SACCOs (www.rca.gov.rw).

The Government of Rwanda resorted to a multi prong strategy. The introduction of Umurenge SACCOs, and side by side expansion of banking network, the development of banking through agents, and taking help of technology to improve access of financial services indeed aided to reduce the level of financial exclusion. Some of the means through which this has been achieved are, improving mobile banking facilities, establishing ATMs at locations where bank branches are not present and encouraging the use of mobile money. We refer to again a FinScope[10] Survey conducted in 2012, which highlighted that that there is a doubling of the percentage of population who accessed formal financial services. In fact from a megre 21% it has increased to as high as 42% and more notably the proportion of population who were entirely excluded from the formal financial institution has reduced by almost 50%; more precisely from 52 to 28% during the period of 2008–2012 (Kavugizo 2014).

The motive behind propagating SACCO, developed in the model of cooperatives, by the Rwandan government rather than other types of financial intermediaries are the following. First, non-financial cooperatives were present in Rwanda for quite some time, as a result of which people had knowledge about functioning of cooperative institutions. Keeping that in view SACCOs are planned as cooperatives institutions that are member based and monitored and supervised by the National Bank of Rwanda (Financial Sector Development Secretariat 2010). This, the authorities perceived, would help people to accept and use the institution better. Secondly, as the cooperative institutions are member centric who in turn governs them, it was felt that people would have a feeling of ownership of the SACCOs. The population of Rwanda primarily fall in low income category and hence low level of capital requisite for SACCOs make them affordable to many (Ephraim 2014).

[10]FinScope is a research tool which was developed by FinMark Trust 2 in an effort to address the need for credible financial sector information to provide guidance in terms of how to respond to some of the challenges policy makers, regulators and financial service providers are faced with.

In addition to involving local level governance system, to begin with, certain infrastructural requirements of SACCOs are addressed by the Government subsequently by making available some space for starting their operations. Later they were helped to acquire land and construct premises by the state. It was also felt that financial literacy of the general population is necessary and attempts had been made to improve the same. Side by side training programmes were organised to improve the knowledge of the staffs working in SACCOs. Initial handholding also involved providing of subsidy to the SACCOs on a temporary basis. Once a SACCO could break even such subsidies were discontinued (Financial Sector Development Secretariat 2010).

Thus to conclude, when the first FinScope Rwanda survey was taken up in 2008 (see National Institute of Statistics of Rwanda (2012)) it uncovered that as high as 79% of adult (18 years or more) population of Rwanda were outside the formal financial institutions in terms of usage of the services. This also indicates that a large amount of funds probably are kept in informal saving institutions or at home and not channelized to the mainstream financial institutions. Such findings provided a signal to the Government that accessible financial institutions are necessary in the country which the poor can easily make use of and justified the intervention such as Umurenge SACCO program (Bosire et al. 2014).

The subsequent Finscope survey (2012) showed the fruitful results of such interventions as the usage of formal financial services by adults doubled (Kavugizo 2014), showing significant improvement in financial inclusion in the country.

3.3.2 A Technology Based Model and Its Success Story in Kenya

Technology can be a great aid to financial inclusion as is evidenced by the MPESA initiative of Kenya. M-PESA is an example of how mobile-based services can aid the excluded section, but also operate as a channel for helping over all development of the nation. Safaricom, a mobile service provider played a crucial role to bring financial inclusion in Kenya. This is done by a mobile service provider in Kenya, namely Safaricom. Under this initiative electronic accounts were opened for a large number of especially excluded customers and an SMS based money transfer system was put in place. This has helped to deposit, withdraw or carry out other essential banking services by the hitherto excluded population using mobile phones. The drive was known as M-PESA, where M stands for mobile and Pesa for the 'money', was considered as one of the successful financial inclusion drives using technology (Ondiege 2012). Within a span of 2 years from 2007 to 2009 the impact of the initiative grew rapidly covering large number of people by reaching to around 65% of Kenyan households (Mas et al. 2011). As of December 2011, through this initiative around US$1.37 billion equivalent currency could be transferred, and recorded as high as 40.01 million transactions. Some studies also report substantial income increase, to the tune of 5 to 30% due to the use of MPESA. There were other benefits as well. Further, a reliable mobile-payments platform has aided and motivated several start-ups in Nairobi, and helped to increase employment and income (The Economist 2013).

Needless to say, prior to the 2007 launch, Safaricom had carried out necessary preparations and a number of essential investments were made. The first was to ensure availability of large number of agents; more precisely they created 750 M-PESA providers nation-wide, and made sure that at least one M-PESA agent was available in each of Kenya's 69 districts. Together with such wide spread supply network, a nationwide advertising campaign was carried out with a view to enhance demand. This was found necessary to build trust and convince people that their limited resources are in safe hands. Thus, Safaricom had a huge market share when the service was launched which ensured financial inclusion of millions of potential users (Alliance for Financial Inclusion 2011). As the technology made cash withdrawal, transfer and payments easier, the scope of MPESA also broadened over time. Many workers working in the urban areas used to send money to their families located in the rural regions and the easy transfer of remittance through this initiative helped to satisfy the needs of the urban customers (Mas and Radcliffe 2011). The rural Kenyans too hailed this programme as they no longer needed to travel long distances which in turn saved their transactions costs substantially. Reducing the procedural complications is another major advantage which made this product popular among the poor (Mas et al. 2011). It was reported in January, 2015 by the GSMA mobile money for the unbanked programme that out of the 33 million Kenyans who owned mobile phones, 26.7 million had registered mobile transfer service accounts. Such significant coverage is particularly noteworthy (Muthiora 2015). An important attraction of M-PESA is its low cost (estimated in terms of US dollar at around US$0.38–0.44 per transaction), and therefore it is not surprising that the initiative have led to a substantial increase (58% to be precise) in the number of Kenyans who own bank accounts. Financial intermediation, as economic theory tells us helps to enhance income and growth and this seems to happen in Kenya with many otherwise excluded sections of population benefitting from the initiative. After observing such results MPESA initiative was considered as a successful endeavour worth emulating by other developing nations across the world (Jack et al. 2010).

Thus within a short span of time, by the use of technology, Kenya has been able to make significant changes in terms of reducing financial exclusion. Certain statistics may help elucidate the achievements. As low as 26% adults in the country had access to formal financial sector during 2006, which had more than doubled in a span of less than ten years to reach the figure of 66.7% by 2013 (World Council of Credit Unions, "Using mobile technology to expand financial inclusion". https://www.woccu.org/documents/WOCCUTechnicalGuide_MobileTechnology). This entire endeavour was well supported by the Central Bank of Kenya which helped to arrive at a socially desirable outcome.

Many felt that the Central bank of Kenya took a bold step towards ensuring financial inclusion even through a non banking institution (Rosengard 2016). By taking aid of technology it made clear its commitment towards ensuring an efficient payment network together with adequately mitigating operational, legal, and liquidity risks. The Central bank thus became a role model by showing how one can ensure financial intermediation for the poor and thereby enhance their livelihood possibilities and income (Rosengard 2016).

3.3.3 Improving Financial Inclusion Through Mzansi Accounts in South Africa

South Africa has often been characterized by a marked economic, social, and political dichotomy. The problem of apartheid between the Caucasians and the indigenous population continued until 1994, after which a political revolution placed into power the African National Congress (ANC) that sought to abolish the system of apartheid and bring balance between the two communities. Pre-1994, the financial sector and related government policies were focused towards the benefit of only a small portion of the population, and had disenfranchised a majority of the population from participating in the financial system effectively. Owing to this, the ANC identified financial inclusion as one of the vital aspects towards better social integration of previously marginalized communities (AFI Group 2014).

The banking sector of South Africa is privately owned and well developed, having access to significant infrastructural and operational resources, and is dominated by four major commercial banks that together account for 90% of the market share. Due to this structure, few innovations and policies were undertaken to assist lower income segments of South African society. State owned financial enterprises do not have a significant presence, and only the financial extension of the Post Office, Postbank, is a significant provider of financial services (AFI Group 2014).

Owing to this, even a decade after reforms in 2004, there was a distinct lack of financial inclusion in the country. Data from the Finmark Trust indicate that 42.3% of the population was 'unbanked', that is, had never participated in the banking sector, and a further 12.3% were previously banked (FinMark Trust Finscope 2004). These results indicate that more than half of South Africans were currently not banked as of that year. In addition, the survey revealed that the unbanked were most prevalent across households with relatively low incomes and living standards.

This lack of financial inclusion had become a source of growing concerns, especially for policy makers who were dedicated to correcting the economic and social imbalances that had been propagated throughout the nation's history. In response, a Financial Sector Charter (FSC) was constituted in 2004 as a pact between the different stakeholders in the financial system: the government, private companies, labor, and civil society. The charter in which, membership though voluntary, was held by most financial institutions, set targets for members in terms of financial inclusion (including access and literacy). If targets were satisfactorily met by a member, the institution (bank) would be better favoured to receive state contracts and related business (AFI Group 2014).

In order to most effectively meet these targets, member institutions opted to combine efforts and offer a series of basic financial services under a single easily recognizable brand. Collaboration was undertaken so as to alleviate the issue of a lack of knowledge of low income markets, and in order to share the extensive advertising costs of the associated campaign to expand financial literacy among the unbanked (AFI Group 2014).

The four major banks and the Postbank were the collaborators for providing the basic, or Mzansi account. However, due to the nature of the South African competition policy, pricing and product features of Mzansi accounts had to be determined individually. Instead, the collaboration agreed upon some basic principles upon which the offered services would be based. These included the omission of interbank transactions costs (which were reimbursed through removal of such interbank fees) and several other costs and transactions fees for Mzansi account holders, the use of a single brand, and the use of a single debit card for operations of these accounts (AFI Group 2014). In addition, only the national ID card was required in order to open an account, which allowed those with little formal documentation to enter the banking system easily (Kristen 2006). Initially, however, severe restrictions were placed upon the volume of transactions and account values that such accounts were eligible for, but were later removed due to reduced revenues resulting from these restrictions (AFI Group 2014).

The Postbank initially acted as an issuing bank, and then gradually converted their accounts into Mzansi accounts in order to take advantage of the reduced interbank fees and other bank ATMs (the Postbank owned no ATMs).

The reception of Mzansi accounts was stellar, with the number of accounts that were opened growing near exponentially from 1.4 million in 2005 to 4.5 million in 2010 (The Banking Association of South Africa 2011). Porteous (2007) further shows that the contribution of Postbank account conversion to this increase is minimal to the degree of new account opening. By 2008, data collected by the FinMark Trust's FinScope 2008 indicated that the proportion of unbanked had reduced to 29.8%, and the proportion of banked had increased to 62.7%. That is, an additional 17.7% of the population had been inducted into the banking system in just four years. Data from the Banking Association of South Africa indicate that 91.3% of Mzansi account holders are new to the bank in which their account was opened. Sixty-two percent of account holders were aged between 25 and 54 years, and indigenous communities account for most of the newly opened accounts (Kirsten 2006).

However, this increase in banking inclusion had been accompanied by active awareness and financial education programs that had helped improve the success of the Mzansi initiative considerably. By 2007, upon observing a relatively high percentage of inactive users, banks launched a more targeted series of awareness campaigns and sales efforts, which increased the proportion of active users to 82% by 2010 (AFI Group 2014).

The agenda of financial inclusion in South Africa has been characterized by an effective incentive structure for private agents, coupled with active and dynamic efforts to improve banking for low income groups. Perhaps these features of the policy are responsible for a large part of the success of the initiative.

3.4 Conclusion

On the global platform various institutions including banks, non-banking financial institutions, businesses and the government are attempting to widen the network of people having access to formal financial tools by reaching out to the traditionally unserved populations through largely non-traditional tools. The gains from increasing financial inclusion have been substantial, and realising this, some developing countries have made substantial progress in addressing some of the key barriers.

We have discussed how MPESA initiative in Kenya brought through non banking institution has been successful in ensuring financial inclusion of the poor and enhancing their income. Banking correspondent models are also seen to be success especially when adopted together with modern technology and examples are present from South Asia and Latin America. Other initiatives that are technology based include mobile wallets, pre-paid cards, biometric ATMs and kiosks; these are low cost products and because of the wide spread use of mobile telephones, these products can be used by the masses of rural and urban areas today.

Several measures to improve financial inclusion are under way. While many efforts have been widely successful some have shown only modest results. There is still much to do, but efforts taken by countries look promising and should enable them to move a step closer towards the goal of wider financial inclusion.

Like other emerging and developing nations, India has also taken a number of measures to improve financial inclusion of the poor; some are successful and some still need further thrust to be useful to the poor. As mentioned we have visited some of the regions in the state of Karnataka to understand the nature of the problems faced by the urban self employed. However, before going to discuss such field level experiences, it is useful to have an idea of accessibility of financial resources especially by the poor at the macro level, for the country as a whole as well as state-wise. As mentioned above, NSSO Debt and Investment Survey (2013) has come up with an account of accessibility to credit by the households through a large survey comprising more than 1 lakh households across the country. As this report provides several valuable indicators of accessibility to financial services by the poorer sections of the society, it is useful to analyse NSSO data concentrating especially on the urban households.

References

AFI Financial Inclusion Data Working Group and the National Treasury, South Africa (2014) The Mzansi Story and Beyond, The Use of Financial Inclusion Data Country Case Study: SOUTH AFRICA, January 2014

Aggarwal S, Klapper L (2013) Designing government policies to expand financial inclusion: Evidence from around the world. Unpublished working paper, World Bank, Washington, DC

Alliance for Financial Inclusion (2011) Mobile financial services and financial inclusion. Africa Growth Initiative at the Brookings Institution, Washington D.C. http://www.afi-global.org/

Atkinson A, Messy F (2013) Promoting financial inclusion through financial education: OECD/INFE evidence, policies and practice. In: OECD working papers on finance, insurance and private pensions, No. 34, OECD Publishing

Bansal A (2012) Profitable models for financial inclusion. Global J Manage Res. Oct-Dec. 1–9

Beck T, Demirgüç-Kunt A, Ross L (2007) Finance, inequality and the poor. J Econ Growth. Springer 12(1):27–49

CGAP (2009) Financial access: Measuring access to financial services around the world. Consultative group to assist the poor. The World Bank, Washington DC

CGAP/World Bank (2010) Financial access 2010. The State of Financial Inclusion through the Crisis. www.cgap.org

Crépon B, Devoto F, Duflo E, Parienté W (2011) Impact of microcredit in rural areas of Morocco: evidence from a randomized evaluation. MIT Working Paper

Demirgüç-Kunt A, Klapper L (2013) Measuring financial inclusion: explaining variation in use of financial services across and within countries. Brookings Pap Econ Act 2013(1):279–340

Demirguc-Kunt A, Klapper L, Singer D, Van Oudheusden P (2015) The global findex database 2014: measuring financial inclusion around the world Policy Research Working Paper No. 7255, The World Bank Group

Donovan K (2012) Mobile money for financial inclusion. Information and communication for development, pp 61–73. The World Bank, Washington D.C

Ephraim Rugazura (2014) Rwanda targeting 80 per cent financial inclusion in 2017.International Journal of Management and Social Sciences Research . Vol. 3, No. 9, September

European Commission (2011) Commission recommendation on access to a basic payment account. European Commission, Brussels

Financial Sector Development Secretariat (2010) "Umurenge SACCOs strategy". Ministry of Finance and Economic Planning, Government of Rwanda. http://www.rca.gov.rw/IMG/pdf/Umurenge_SACCOs_strategy_February09.pdf

Forbes (2011) Financial inclusion models from around the world. Forbes India Magazine, November 2010 edition. http://forbesindia.com/article/financial-inclusion/financial-inclusion-models-from-around-the-world/19292/1

Goldberg J (2014) Products and policies to promote saving in developing countries. IZA World of Labor. http://wol.iza.org/articles/products-and-policies-to-promote-saving-in-developing-countries.pdf

Huefner F, Bykere A (2015) Financial inclusion: a financial industry perspective. The Institute of International Finance

Jack W, Suri T (2010) The economics of M-Pesa. MIT Sloan, Massachusetts

Johnston D, Morduch J (2008) The unbanked: evidence from Indonesia. World Bank Econ Rev 22(3):517–537

Josephat BK, Iyikirenga MR, Msaki, Leonard Juda (2014) Umurenge SACCO as a tool for financial inclusion. Int J Inf Technol Bus Manage 29(1)

Judah S (2013) Making time: helping child workers save their earnings. BBC News Magazine. http://www.bbc.com/news/magazine-24281511

Kavugizo K (2014) Rwanda's financial inclusion success story. Alliance for financial inclusion. http://www.afiglobal.org/sites/default/files/publications/afi_case_study_rwanda_finalweb.pdf

Kendall J, Mylenko N, Ponce A (2010) Measuring financial access around the world, World Bank Policy Research Working Paper No. 5253, The World Bank

Kirsten M (2006) Policy initiatives to expand financial outreach in South Africa. Paper delivered at World Bank/Brookings Institute Conference, May 2006

Lusardi A, Mitchell O (2011) Financial literacy around the world: an overview. NBER Working Paper No. 17107

Mas I, Radcliffe D (2011) Mobile payments go viral: M-Pesa in Kenya. Journal of financial transformation, Vol. 32, Pg 169–182

Mettenheim K (2013) New perspectives on banking and agendas for financial inclusion. Doctoral dissertation, Harvard Kennedy School Cambridge Massachusetts

Muthiora B (2015) Enabling mobile money policies in Kenya. Groupe Speciale Mobile Association, London

National Institute of Statistics of Rwanda (2012) FinScope survey report: Financial inclusion in rwanda 2008–2012, Rwanda

National Sample Survey Organization (NSSO) (2013) All India debt and investment survey, NSSO, New Delhi

Ondiege P (2012) Fostering financial inclusion with mobile banking. Private sector and development. http://www.proparco.fr/jahia/webdav/site/proparco/shared/PORTAILS/Secteur_prive_developpement/PDF/SPD16/SPD16_Peter_Ondiege_UK.pdf

Porteous D (2007) Just how transformational is M-banking? Fin Mark Trust

Robinson M (2004) Why the bank Rakyat Indonesia has the World's largest sustainable micro-banking system. In: BRI International Seminar, Bali, Indonesia. http://www.ruralfinance.org/fileadmin/templates/rflc/documents/1117473611572_Robinson_BRI_Paper_Revised_April_2005.pdf

Rosengard JK (2016) A quantum leap over high hurdles to financial inclusion: the mobile banking revolution in Kenya. SWIFT Institute working paper No. 2015-005

The Banking Association South Africa (2011) Annual Review 2011, Parktown. www.banking.org.za

The Economist (2013) Why does Kenya lead the world in mobile banking

Triki T, Faye I (2013) Financial inclusion in Africa. African Development Bank, Tunisia

UNSGSA (2014) Financial inclusion: a path to empowerment and opportunity. Annual Report to the Secretary General

World Bank (2011).Gender equity as smart economics-a world bank group gender action plan

World Bank (2012) General Guidelines for the development of government payment programs. World Bank, Washington, DCWorld Bank (2014) Global financial development report 2014: Financial inclusion. World Bank, Washington, DC

World Bank (2014) Global financial development report 2014: Financial inclusion. World Bank, Washington, DC

Chapter 4
Credit Access of Urban Households: A Study of NSSO Data

4.1 Introduction

From the global experiences we now focus on India by first highlighting some of the macroeconomic indicators observed in case of access to financial services in general and credit in particular. In the context of financial inclusion while opening of a bank account is the first step, access to credit is of paramount importance in a nation where large percentage of households are self employed either in agriculture or in other occupations. The NSSO data which particularly focuses on the access to credit is therefore heighted in this chapter. As mentioned in Chap. 1 National Sample Survey Organisation (NSSO) provides data on this subject by collecting information at the household level through the Debt and Investment Surveys. We have analysed the unit record data and present some of the findings in this chapter based on the recently published 70th round data as well as statistics from the previous round viz., the 59th round.

The 70th round NSSO survey was conducted during the period January to December 2013 covering the entire Indian Territory with the exception of Andaman & Nicobar Islands, Chandigarh, Dadra & Nagar Haveli and Lakshadweep. As in the case of previous rounds the 70th round also aimed at (i) acquiring statistical information both from rural and urban regions regarding demand for credit as well as (ii) from institutional and non institutional sources data concerning supply of credit. Questionnaire based interviews were carried out to collect data (www.mospi.nic.in).

Data were collected for the following indicators (www.mospi.nic.in):

(i) the asset position of the household as on 30th June 2012, classified in two major categories viz., financial assets and physical assets.
(ii) the liabilities of the households evaluated as on 30th June 2012 in visit 1 and as on 30th June 2013 in visit 2
(iii) in addition the level of capital expenditure on farm and nonfarm activities, residential plots or houses incurred by the household during the one year period of July 2012–June 2013.

M. Rajeev and B.P. Vani, *Financial Access of the Urban Poor in India*, SpringerBriefs in Economics, DOI 10.1007/978-81-322-3712-9_4

As mentioned, two visits were made by NSSO personals to collect information; during 2013 first visit was completed starting from January and ending in July (a total of seven months). The second visit in 2013 was of duration 5 months from August to December. The central sample covered 4529 villages and 3705 urban blocks where visits 1 and 2 covered more or less equal number of households. In particular the questionnaire schedule was administered for 62,135 households in rural areas and 48,665 in urban regions in visit1. In visit 2, during August to December rural househols covered were 61,650 and the figure for urban stood at 46,771. A fixed reference period (viz., 30th June, 2012) was used to assess the position of assets and liabilities of the sample households and the information provided by the respondents was noted. As the survey was a repeat survey comparability issue was also kept in mind.

From this survey by operating on the unit record data, we have separated the data for the urban households and made further analysis. Subsequently we also make a comparison with some of the findings from the previous round data viz., the 59th round. The data set (59th round) also provides information concerning debt and investment position of households covering a total of 1,43,285 households in the country, from both rural and urban regions. Thus these surveys are a source of rich information on household debt and investment situation. But there are not many studies that utilize this large micro level data base for analysis (see Bhatacharjee et al. 2010). Scholars often put forth their arguments based on the data published in NSSO reports only. More importantly, there appears to be not many studies based on the above data set that have dealt with the issue of accessibility to credit by the urban poor.

The NSSO data make available information concerning outstanding loan possessed by a household on a pre-specified date (for example, 30th June, 2002 is for 59th round data). Considering this information at the household level one can compute the percentage of households that have outstanding loan within a given category of households (such as within a social or consumption category). The indicator derived is termed as the incidence of indebtedness (IOI). Certain observations regarding IOI are noteworthy. First, if we carefully examine the indicator we observe that it is higher for the groups that have higher income or more precisely consumption level. Further economically better off states have comparatively higher level of IOI. Concentrating on social categories we observe that schedule tribe (ST) households usually tend to have lower IOI compared to the general or other backward caste (OBC) category of households. These observations lead us to believe that incidence of indebtedness provides an assessment of access to credit rather than being an indicator of distress, though the latter possibility also cannot be entirely eliminated. No doubt accessibility to credit is an important aspect of financial inclusion even though there are other dimensions of financial inclusion such as savings or remittance facilities.

A study of household indebtedness necessitates a look at its various features. On the one hand, indebtedness connotes accessibility to credit and on the other, an outcome of un-paid past loans that indicate distress. Whether indebtedness implies access or distress depends on the terms and conditions of the loan, income of the household, utilization-pattern of the loan and other related factors. The present chapter attempts to explore the nature and extent of indebtedness across households of different characteristics in selected states of India. In addition we also present an analysis of data on borrowings. An exercise of this nature will provide a macro picture on financial intermediation for the urban populace.

Using the recent round (70th) that provide information regarding insurance and deposits and we capture several components of financial inclusion and categories households according to the level of inclusion as not included or completely excluded, partially included and so on. This chapter is subdivided into the following sections: The second section provides the rationale behind the subdivision of households into various classes for the 59th and 70th rounds and Sects. 4.3–4.8 discuss various aspects related to indebtedness. A concluding section is presented at the end.

4.2 Subdivision of Households

To examine whether the nature of indebtedness differs across different households, we subdivided the households according to economic condition, gender of the head of the household and social status. For the 59th round data, households were subdivided into three different classes based on monthly per capita consumption expenditures (MPCEs): Rs 0–500, Rs 500–1000 and above Rs 1000. In the absence of income data MPCE provides a proxy for economic status of a household. However, MPCE data are not available for the 70th round and such an analysis therefore is not possible for the recent round. As far as social classes are concerned, as per information provided by NSSO, Scheduled Caste, Scheduled Tribe and general category households are considered separately. Analyses were also carried out separately for male-headed and female-headed households.[1]

4.3 Indebtedness of Households: Selected State-Wise Comparison

As already mentioned, NSSO data provide information regarding households that have outstanding loans on a pre-specified date (for example, in case of 59th round it was June 30, 2002). Based on this information at the household level, we can arrive at the percentage of households belonging to a particular economic or

[1]If the head of the household is a male, the household is considered as male-headed household by NSSO, while the female-headed households are those, which are headed by a female member.

Table 4.1 Incidence of indebtedness by monthly per capita consumption expenditures (MPCEs) in urban and rural areas of each state (from both formal and informal sources) (percentages)

MPCE (Rupees)	Urban					
	MP	Chhattisgarh	Punjab	Haryana	WB	Karnataka
0–500	17.1	10.2	18.2	23.6	20	11.3
500–1000	14.4	13.9	12.5	16.3	16.4	20.9
Above	21.7	18.1	12.5	12.7	15.7	20.2
All	17.7	13.2	13.1	16	17.1	18.6
MPCE (Rupees)	*Rural*					
	MP	*Chhattisgarh*	*Punjab*	*Haryana*	*WB*	*Karnataka*
0–500	25.3[a]	18.8	26.2	31.9	20.1	27.9
500–1000	29.6	25.7	25.8	25.8	25.1	37.6
Above	34.9	28	27.2	13	34.9	31.4
All	26.2	19.8	25.7	27.3	21.8	31.3

[a]25.3% of the households in the MPCE class 0–500 in rural areas of MP were having loan outstanding as on 30.06.02

MP: Madhya Pradesh, WB: West Bengal

Source Computed by authors using 59th round NSSO, All India Debt and Investment Survey (AIDIS)

social category that have outstanding credit. This indicator is termed as the incidence of indebtedness (IOI) and is considered as an indicator of access to credit rather than distress (Basu 2006; Rajeev et al. 2011). However, the latter possibility also cannot be ruled out especially for the relatively poorer households (Basu 2006).

Our analysis of unit record data reveals that incidence of indebtedness in urban areas is around 10.2% (not shown in the table). Table 4.1 clearly shows that access to credit in rural areas is far higher than in urban regions. Secondly, the poorer households in developed regions in urban areas have better access to credit vis-a-vis the less developed and middle performing ones (Table 4.1). For instance, IOI for the poorest category of households in the urban areas of Haryana, a developed state, is 23.6%, where as for West Bengal, a middle performing state, it is 20%, while it is a mere 10.2% for Chhattisgarh.

One may argue in this context that in the urban areas, indebtedness may be lower due to lack of demand for credit. As information on demand is not directly available, it is useful to analyze the data using occupation wise classifications under the assumption that the households depending on self-employment (farm or non-farm) would need regular flow of credit to fund their business activities. This is particularly so as about 80% of urban households in this sample are with MPCE below Rs. 630. Thus assuming a households of size 5, monthly expenditure for the household may be estimated to be around Rs 3000 which is rather low.[2] Thus one

[2]For the rural households about 75% of households in the NSSO 59th round sample are with MPCE less than Rs 600.

Table 4.2 Incidence of indebtedness (IOI) of self-employed households in urban and rural areas of different states (both formal and informal sources)

State	Urban	Rural
Chhattisgarh	17.5	23.3
Madhya Pradesh (MP)	15.4	32
Punjab	11.9	30
Haryana	17.7	33.3
West Bengal (WB)	15.6	23.8
Karnataka	19.8	38

Source Computed by authors using 59th round NSSO, All India Debt and Investment Survey (AIDIS)

may not expect savings from these households to be invested in their business.[3] In this regard, our occupation-wise analysis of self employed households further strengthens our assertion (see Table 4.2).

A comparison of IOI in urban areas across states (see Table 4.2) that considered only the self-employed households into account, has revealed that differences in access to credit still persists across the states. More importantly, difference is substantial between urban and rural households as revealed by the comparison. Taken state-wise, it is seen that Incidence of Indebtedness is greater in Karnataka as compared with other states; more precisely, 19.8% self-employed households in Karnataka have access to credit, followed by Haryana and Chhattisgarh with 17.7 and 17.5% respectively. Thus, accessibility to credit is better in urban regions of Karnataka compared to urban regions in other Indian states, while rural credit accessibility remains much higher than urban.

The question that arises now is whether the differences in accessibility to credit, evident from the incidence of indebtedness, are due to differences in access to credit from formal lending agencies or due to the development of informal credit market in a region. Providing an answer to this question lies in separating the share of loans from formal lending agencies in the total number of loans outstanding.

4.4 Sources of Credit: Extent of Exclusion

A disaggregated analysis of the sources of credit presented in Table 4.3 reveals that households with comparatively better economic status enjoy higher access to credit from the formal sector both in rural and urban areas. It is further observed that most

[3]One of our earlier surveys relating to the Karnataka farmers shows that 75% of the small and marginal farmers could barely meet their consumption needs. We expect similar situation for the urban poor as well.

Table 4.3 Percentage share of loans availed from the formal lending agencies in total number of loans outstanding (as on 30.06.2002) by Monthly Per Capita Consumption Expenditures (MPCEs) in urban and rural areas of each state (59th round)

MPCE (Rupees)	Urban					
	MP	Chhattisgarh	Punjab	Haryana	WB	Karnataka
0–500	26.9	23	8.3	29.4	24.9	44.2
500–1000	63.4	64.7	28.5	28.8	28.7	52.2
Above 1000	88.9	92	56.1	56.9	72.3	68.4
All	59.1	60.8	33.7	37.6	39.1	56.6
MPCE (Rupees)	*Rural*					
	MP	*Chhattisgarh*	*Punjab*	*Haryana*	*WB*	*Karnataka*
0–500	45	63.6	25.3	36.3	46.3	45.7
500–1000	55.6	76.7	37.3	53.1	46.8	50.6
Above 1000	75.6	71	63.2	80.4	63.8	79.1
All	48.1	65.9	39	47.4	47.5	48.7

MP: Madhya Pradesh, WB: West Bengal
Source Computed by authors using 59th round NSSO, All India Debt and Investment Survey (AIDIS)

of the loans availed by the poorer households in the developed region are from informal sources. For instance, the percent of loan from the formal sector availed by households in the poorest MPCE class in urban areas of Madhya Pradesh was 26.9; in Punjab it was 8.3 and Karnataka it was 44.2. In other words, for the households with monthly per capita consumption below Rs. 500 in Karnataka, 55.8% of the loans came from the informal sources and in Punjab the corresponding percentage was 91.7. The study reveals that higher access to credit in some of the states in India, as evidenced by the higher incidence of indebtedness (Table 4.2), is primarily due to the presence of a well-developed informal lending market.

There could be several reasons behind the regional differences in access to credit from informal sources. One should note that richer households in a region often tend to be informal lenders, and it is possible that due to the poor economic conditions of most of the households in less developed regions, the informal lending market of less developed regions might have fewer lenders. Our analysis of the unit record data of NSSO (AIDIS, 59th Round), reveals that in urban areas of Chhattisgarh, Punjab and Karnataka, respectively 1.4, 1.9 and 1.9 percentages of the households supplied loans (acted as lenders). In West Bengal, Haryana and Madhya Pradesh, the corresponding figures are 6.8, 2.7 and 2.5 percentages respectively. Apart from computing percentage of lender households, we have also computed the ratio of loan suppliers to incidence of indebtedness, displaying percentage of lender per 100 borrowers. From this analysis it is observed that especially in rural areas of less developed regions there are relatively fewer lenders vis-à-vis other regions and therefore plausibly lack of even informal lender in the less developed regions reduces the borrowing opportunity of the poor. In urban regions the situation is mixed.

Table 4.4 Percentage shares of loans availed from the formal lending agencies in total number of loan outstanding (as on 30.06.02) by head of the household in selected states (59th round)

State	Urban		Rural	
	Male headed	Female headed	Male headed	Female headed
Chhattisgarh	61	57.1	64.8	85.8
Madhya Pradesh	61.9	8.6	48.2	43.6
Punjab	35	19.7	41.2	21.5
Haryana	37.6	37.4	47.5	45.2
West Bengal	38.2	49.7	47.9	38.3
Karnataka	59.1	40.2	50.6	30.3
All	49.5	36.3	49.2	36.7

Source Computed by authors using 59th round NSSO, All India Debt and Investment Survey (AIDIS)

Lenders in less developed regions may also be fewer in number due to poorer repayment capability of most of the borrowers, which in turn may have made lending in less developed regions riskier than in developed regions. We have computed the actual repayment figures[4] which reveal that repayment rates are better in urban areas and there are fewer differences across regions. Thus, it is probable that in spite of making timely repayment, the urban poor face problems in accessing credit from informal sources which make their condition more pathetic.

Further, a gender-wise comparison of sources of loan to households has revealed that male-headed households generally avail more loans from formal lending agencies than female-headed households (Table 4.4). Some states may be exceptions; for example, in West Bengal, total loans availed by female-headed households is greater than that of male-headed households, while in Haryana, the loans availed by both male-headed and female-headed households are equal. On the other hand, a comparison of source of loan across households (who borrowed) belonging to different social groups reveals that Scheduled Tribes households avail more loans from formal agencies than households of other social classes. At the All India level while for urban regions 70% of ST households that had borrowed had availed loan from formal agencies, for SC, OBC and general categories the corresponding figures are 38, 46 and 53 respectively. For rural areas access to formal agencies is relatively better as the schedule caste households who could access credit, 46% of them got loan from formal agency. For general category

[4]The All India debt and Investment Survey was carried out by visiting each sample household twice. The first visit was carried out between January and August 2003, while the second visit was from September to December 2003. During the first visit, data was collected on the amount of borrowings and repayments during 1.7.02–31.12.02. During the second visit, information on borrowing and repayment was collected for the period between 1.1.03 and 30.6.03. Using this data, thus one can arrive at percentage of households that borrowed or repaid loans in 2002–03.

households, however, the figure is around the same at 52%. Thus we observe that access to formal loan is lower for certain social classes and especially in urban regions. In Karnataka, OBC households are found to have availed the highest percent share of loans. Possibly a higher share of loans from formal lending agencies to Scheduled Tribe households (who have been able to get access to credit from some sources) is indicative of their lower access to informal moneylenders, and also to their having accessed certain scheme based loans. Stated otherwise, unlike others ST households obtain their credit requirements largely from formal sources.

These findings indicate that there are certain specific categories that need special attention during the financial inclusion drive.

4.5 Terms and Conditions of Loan: Cost of Exclusion (59th Round)

Our analysis shows that access to credit is largely determined by the size of informal lending market in a region and whether the terms and conditions of loan are regulated by the government. A study on indebtedness therefore should also focus on terms and conditions under which loans are available. Moreover, a household may find it difficult to avail as well as repay loans if terms and conditions are unfavorable. An analysis of interest rate with respect to households with MPCE less than Rs 500 reveals that around 45% of households who availed loan paid an interest charge higher than 30%. For Chhattisgarh this figure is as high as 58%. Thus a large section of poorer households are forced to avail loan at an exorbitant interest rate and many poorer states show more adverse terms and condition. But our analysis reveals that for households with MPCE above Rs 1000, only 12% of them are availing loan at 30% or higher rate of interest. Thus the richer households avail even informal loans at better terms and conditions. In regard to differences in interest rate between male-headed and female-headed households, our study could not find any clear-cut difference in interest rate between the two.

From the 59th round we next move to the more recent 70th round data.

4.6 Financial Exclusion in Urban Regions: Recent Macro Scenario from NSSO 70th Round

Unlike the 59th round data which primarily dealt with credit, NSSO 70th round data provide information regarding deposit, credit as well as insurance accounts. Thus it is possible to have a more comprehensive analysis of different components of financial inclusion for urban regions, which is carried out here by considering various types of accounts such as bank, deposit, post office, insurance and loan accounts. Based on the participation in different banking activities we have classified the households in terms of their level of accessibility. More precisely a household is classified as not included if the household does not have any account (all entries are zero); partially included: household has at least one of the accounts (at least one of them is non zero); moderately included: any two or more accounts exist but not having a loan account; fully included: loan account exists and in addition any two or more of the other accounts are there for the household. Results are presented in Table A4.1 in the Appendix which shows percentage of households as total number of households of that category (such as Schedule caste (SC) or others).

Certain observations from this table are worth mentioning. Around 21% schedule caste (SC) households and 15% households from other categories (other than SC) do not have any type of bank account and hence can be termed as financially excluded. Significantly across states for urban areas the figures are more or less similar. This is important given the fact that in urban areas there is wide spread prevalence of banking network and distance to banks should not act as constraint as in the case of rural areas. The important question is, what then preventing the agents to access banking services? We make a modest attempt to address this question based on our field visits. The problem is especially severe for the socially backward classes. Amongst the urban sample households, only 18% has access to credit (see Table A4.1, last column). With regards to the loan account one may argue that not all households demand credit. To examine this issue more appropriately we have, like before, analysed the data disaggregating according to the type of activities one is engaged with. Amongst them the self employed households are the ones who are so called entrepreneurs, trying to have a living possibly due to not getting any better employment opportunities. One may rightly assume that these are own account enterprise owners with low income level and in regular need of funds for their business activities.[5] Our analysis showed that amongst the self employed households too, 13% are fully financially excluded and 20% have access to credit. Our analysis of borrowing related information shows that around 40% of urban self employed have borrowed funds (from formal or informal sources). Thus probably some of the self employed households are accessing credit through informal sources under adverse terms and conditions. To ascertain this we have conducted a disaggregated analysis of sources of funds. It is observed that 54% of credit has come from the formal institutional sources while 46% still is sourced from the informal sources.

Asset possession wise classification is more illuminating (see Table A4.2 in the Appendix). While in the lowest quintile, only 31% of the households possess access to formal sources of credit out of all households that access credit in this quintile, this percentage becomes as high as 73% for the highest quintile borrowers.

[5]See our argument above concerning NSSO 59th round data.

Thus if we compare the 59th and 70th rounds we do not observe much improvements except for the amount of loan per loanee persons which has increased substantially between the two rounds. But as with the 59th round, the recent data also reveal severe inequality in access to financial services especially credit by the poor which is a major concern for a country where a large percentage of the poor are self employed with no savings and regular need of funds for their business activities.

4.7 Concluding Observations

This chapter mainly attempts to examine the nature and extent of accessibility to credit as seen through the incidence of indebtedness, which is taken as one of the important indicators of the level of financial inclusion of households. The analysis is carried out for the households of different economic characteristics in urban areas of selected states. Unit level NSSO data (AIDIS, 59th and 70th Rounds) were used for this purpose. It is observed that urban households appear to face more problems while availing loans and they seem to get fewer loans from both formal and informal lending sources. Access to formal credit is much lower for the poorer households than their richer counterparts and such differences are seen for various social groups as well. Therefore, it is imperative that certain sections of population such as women-headed households, (consisting primarily of widow with small children and engaged self employed activities), as well as certain social classes such as schedule tribes be given special attention in the financial inclusion drive in order to bring them on par with other groups.

Appendix

Table A4.1 Percentage of urban households financially included (according to social categories and level of inclusion)

Percentage of urban households financially included (according to social categories and level of inclusion)												
	Not included			Partially included			Moderately included			Fully included		
	SC/ST	Others	Total	SC/ST	Others	Total	SC/ST	Others	Total	SC/ST	Others	Total
Jammu & Kashmir	30.4	21.4	22.4	3.4	8.9	8.3	54.8	52.4	52.7	11.4	17.3	16.7
Himachal Pradesh	9.5	5.3	6.1	3.2	1.1	1.5	68.2	74.4	73.2	19.1	19.3	19.3
Punjab	26.8	16.4	19.4	3.9	3.3	3.5	61.2	70.0	67.5	8.0	10.3	9.7
Uttaranchal	23.7	10.0	11.1	0.3	0.5	0.5	57.8	80.5	78.6	18.2	9.0	9.8
Haryana	27.8	24.9	25.3	6.2	3.3	3.7	56.4	63.6	62.5	9.6	8.3	8.5
Delhi	21.8	13.2	14.9	4.3	7.9	7.2	71.8	75.1	74.4	2.2	3.8	3.4
Rajasthan	25.1	18.9	20.4	11.9	5.9	7.4	50.6	64.1	60.8	12.4	11.1	11.4
Uttar Pradesh	25.1	20.0	20.8	5.8	6.3	6.2	60.2	63.8	63.2	8.8	10.0	9.8
Bihar	24.3	31.1	30.1	5.5	11.2	10.4	63.3	50.1	52.1	7.0	7.6	7.5
Assam	16.3	13.9	14.4	3.6	2.7	2.9	51.5	65.1	62.3	28.6	18.3	20.4
West Bengal	20.2	16.2	17.1	11.0	9.5	9.8	54.5	61.2	59.8	14.3	13.1	13.3
Jharkhand	32.6	18.7	22.6	7.9	3.3	4.6	50.9	64.4	60.5	8.7	13.6	12.2
Odisha	37.6	15.0	21.1	9.2	3.6	5.1	39.1	64.8	58.0	14.0	16.6	15.9
Chhattisgarh	40.5	26.7	30.9	11.5	4.3	6.5	42.4	59.1	54.0	5.6	10.0	8.6
Madhya Pradesh	20.2	17.9	18.4	7.7	7.3	7.4	57.8	60.6	60.0	14.3	14.1	14.1
Gujarat	26.9	16.5	18.1	12.9	14.0	13.8	50.5	54.9	54.2	9.7	14.7	13.9
Maharashtra	11.1	9.6	9.8	22.3	11.6	13.3	55.4	64.0	62.7	11.2	14.8	14.2
Andhra Pradesh	15.2	10.8	11.6	7.2	10.0	9.5	44.5	44.3	44.3	33.1	34.9	34.6

(continued)

Table A4.1 (continued)

Percentage of urban households financially included (according to social categories and level of inclusion)												
	Not included			Partially included			Moderately included			Fully included		
	SC/ST	Others	Total	SC/ST	Others	Total	SC/ST	Others	Total	SC/ST	Others	Total
Karnataka	15.2	10.9	11.5	12.1	11.1	11.2	47.6	58.3	56.9	25.0	19.7	20.4
Goa	0.0	6.3	5.9	0.0	17.3	16.2	83.6	58.5	60.1	16.4	17.9	17.8
Kerala	7.7	5.1	5.3	7.7	3.5	3.8	25.7	37.2	36.4	58.9	54.2	54.5
Tamil Nadu	21.9	13.9	15.1	8.8	7.5	7.7	36.4	43.3	42.3	32.8	35.3	34.9
Puducherry	2.6	9.9	9.6	0.0	1.5	1.4	15.9	49.7	48.2	81.5	38.9	40.8
Telengana	18.7	11.0	12.3	31.0	21.7	23.2	35.3	54.6	51.5	15.1	12.6	13.0
All India	21.4	14.9	16.0	10.9	8.9	9.3	52.0	57.8	56.8	15.7	18.4	18.0

Different types of account considered here are Bank account, Deposit account, post office account, insurance account and loan account. Not included: All are zero; Partially included: At least one of them is non zero; Moderately included: Any two or more non zero except loan account; Fully included: loan account and any two or more of the other account is non zero

Source Authors' analysis of NSSO 70th round data

Table A4.2 Share of loans out of total borrowings from formal sources, state wise and asset holding wise classification

	First quintile	Second quintile	Third quintile	Fourth quintile	Last quintile	Total
Jammu & Kashmir	8.7	34.4	32.6	65.3	79.5	62.6
Himachal Pradesh	7.8	37.9	81.2	94.3	85.8	83.1
Punjab	10.0	19.4	31.6	47.7	74.3	39.3
Uttaranchal	35.0	31.7	21.6	62.6	98.8	53.4
Haryana	39.3	38.4	36.8	46.2	83.1	58.2
Delhi	0.6	11.2	49.5	57.3	85.4	44.8
Rajasthan	11.4	20.1	25.4	43.7	68.1	34.5
Uttar Pradesh	13.9	21.5	23.9	40.4	74.8	37.4
Bihar	10.1	25.5	36.8	35.0	58.0	35.1
Assam	56.7	51.6	64.4	78.9	84.7	72.3
West Bengal	23.3	55.2	55.9	64.6	78.9	56.9
Jharkhand	15.0	63.2	62.6	45.4	65.3	55.7
Odisha	54.0	44.7	47.0	57.4	72.4	56.1
Chhattisgarh	6.0	38.2	39.9	29.7	75.2	40.7
Madhya Pradesh	43.1	41.5	46.8	55.3	83.8	56.2
Gujarat	47.4	24.1	47.9	68.3	89.2	60.0
Maharashtra	29.8	57.9	59.8	73.1	90.5	67.7
Andhra Pradesh	16.6	36.1	43.5	45.3	57.8	44.0
Karnataka	33.9	41.1	51.0	61.0	70.4	55.3
Goa	45.1	81.9	82.3	94.6	100.0	85.5
Kerala	59.2	68.9	76.5	79.9	75.5	72.7
Tamil Nadu	36.8	44.3	55.5	60.8	68.6	56.0
Puducherry	30.5	32.2	63.8	78.3	70.3	54.2
Telengana	17.2	31.8	42.9	48.9	63.2	41.9
All India	31.7	41.6	51.1	58.3	72.9	53.9

Source Authors' analysis of NSSO 70th round data

References

Basu P (2006) Improving access to india's rural poor. The World Bank, Washington DC

Bhattacharjee M, Rajeev M (2010) Interest rate formation in informal credit market: does level of development matter? Brooks World Poverty Institute Working Paper No 126, University of Manchester, UK, http://www.bwpi.manchester.ac.uk/resources/Working-Papers/bwpi-wp-12610.pdf

Rajeev M, Vani BP (2011) Farm sector in Karnataka: farmers' indebtedness and risk management, Project No. CESP/93, Institute for Social and Economic Change, Bengaluru

Chapter 5
Understanding Financial Exclusion from the Ground: Survey Methods

While NSSO data contain an overall macro view about urban financial exclusion in terms of accessibility to credit and other services, a field survey was considered necessary to get a clear and more recent picture of the ground reality that especially throws light on the problems perceived by the economic agents in accessing formal services in a sustained manner.

5.1 Selection of Sample

In order to understand the extent and nature of financial exclusion we have selected Karnataka state for our study since financial inclusion drive for the rural areas was carried out here for a long time with some measure of success. Experiences of states that have achieved better financial inclusion will no doubt be of use to the rest of India. On the other hand if we observe that even for such a region, financial inclusion for the urban poor has been lagging behind, it would provide lessons for the other regions where the status of financial inclusion may be much worse. A poor performing state on the other hand may demonstrate features that are not relevant for other regions; or, valid only for regions that display similar characteristics as the former. In this chapter also we attempt to draw certain lessons from the other countries across the globe.

Within the state of Karnataka we have selected Bengaluru urban district, wherein three important markets are taken up for study. The most important market in Bengaluru city is K.R Market, popularly known as the "City Market" or more simply as the "Market". Two other major markets selected from the city are, K.R Puram Market and Jaynagar Market. Though K.R Puram Market is an old market its features have been changing overtime due to the development of the information technology (IT) sector in the region. Given the changing character of the market and its emerging cliental of so called "techies," this market is considered important for the study. Jayanagar market is another old and established market in Bengaluru city which caters to the traditional middle income population.

M. Rajeev and B.P. Vani, *Financial Access of the Urban Poor in India*, SpringerBriefs in Economics, DOI 10.1007/978-81-322-3712-9_5

To select the samples, first, a list of traders operating in a market is collected from the respective (ward) municipal office and then a sample of 100 traders is selected from each market. Missing respondents are replaced by newly selected (randomly selected without replacement) traders from the list. Bengaluru Urban district is in much higher state of development. In order to get the picture of a comparatively less developed district, we added Tumkur district also to our study sample by selecting two important markets from the district, i.e., one from Tumkur taluk and the other from Gubbi Taluk. Similarly, 100 respondents each are selected from two major markets of Tumkur, making a total of 500 respondents. While this survey has given us the demand side scenario, in order to understand the problems from the supply side, we have also held discussions with the lenders of different kinds including banks (both public and private), trader cum lenders and private money lending agencies. The survey was conducted during 2012 and our visits continued thereafter and the recent visits were made during 2016; however, not much difference has been observed over the period. Needless to say, we are not attempting to predict population parameters based on these surveys but attempting to understand the problems of financial intermediations faced by some of the self employed urban poor.

5.2 A Brief Note on Three Sample Markets from Bengaluru[1]

5.2.1 K.R Market

Named after a celebrated King of Mysore State, Maharaj Krishnaraja Wodeyar IV, K.R Market or, better known as City market is a rather large and one of the oldest markets in the city of Bengaluru (see Fig. 5.1). Though this market is primarily a wholesale market, smaller traders also do retail business in city market. Thus large and small including tiny traders sitting in the pavements earn their livelihood in this trading place. Items sold in the market are also numerous-from flower, fruits and vegetables to hardware and clothing. Traders of all religion and

[1]While writing this chapter we have taken help of the following websites.
Source:http://www.nowpublic.com/Bengaluru_city_market_vibrance_and_life_#ixzz2BXvAuMP7
Source: http://www.iijnm.org/media_uploads/thesoftcopy/2011_2012/city_market.html
Source:http://www.myBengaluru.com/article/0810/jayanagar-4th-block-complex-whats-great-about-it-everything.html
Source: http://blogpourri.blogspot.in/2005/09/life-in-Bengaluru-local-market-preps.html
Source: http://www.deccanherald.com/content/265010/a-landmark-ready-disappear.html
Source: http://www.tumkurlife.com/
Source: http://164.100.52.24/pdf/karnataka/District%20Profiles/Tumkur.pdf
Source: http://www.advantagekarnataka.com/images/district-profiles/Tumkur-District-Profile.pdf.

Fig. 5.1 A view of city market. Photos taken by the authors

Source for the map:www.google.co.in/maps

Fig. 5.1 (continued)

social classes are present in the market, consisting of large number of women traders as well. Thus this market is considered an ideal location to study a variety of traders.

5.2.2 K.R. Puram Market

Krishnarajapurm Market has a history of about 250 years, dating back to the 19th Century. This was inaugurated by then Maharaja of Mysore dynasty. It was in the year 1995 that BBMP constructed 112 shops and later allotted to local traders; but still many do business in makeshift type of sheds (Fig. 5.2). In addition, about 25 slaughter houses and 20 commercial complexes are located around this market. According to Trader's Association (Karnataka farmers and traders Association, K.R. Puram), as on December 2010, about 450 street vendors were operating in this market and about one thousand farmers were dependent on this market for sale of their produces. A majority of them are engaged in vegetables trading business, followed by flower and fruit vending. This market is well known for a weekly fair which is conducted on every Tuesday. More than 150 vendors earn their livelihood by selling flowers at the market every day. Some customers visit the market on a daily basis, some come thrice a week and some twice a month. Customers at this market, by and large are from the upper middle class group. Other bulk customers at the market are from the hotel industry which caters to the needs of people working in the IT and other industries in Bengaluru (Fig. 5.2).

Fig. 5.2 K.R Puram market. Photos taken by the authors

K.R.PURAM Market Map - Location of target respondents

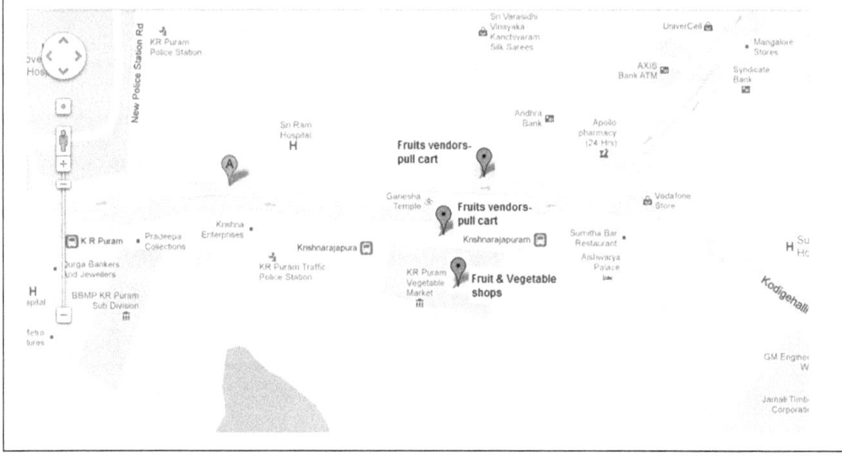

Source for the map:www.google.co.in/maps

Fig. 5.2 (continued)

Changing Nature of K.R. Puram Market: Insights from Survey

According to Mr. Ramappa, the present secretary of trader's association who has been carrying out vegetable and other allied business since the past 25 years and also a former farmer himself, there has been a significant development/improvement both in terms of number of farmers approaching this market vis-a-vis the people accessing this market from 2005 onwards, thanks to a judgment of the Hon'ble High court of Karnataka. As explained earlier, vegetables and flowers that come to K.R. Puram Market are from the taluks of Bengaluru Rural district as well as the neighbouring district of Kolar. There are a few major lakes in these taluks (district subdivision) from which earlier water was allowed to flow through crust gates into agricultural lands below. In the past there were many instances of excess water draining out from these agricultural lands of which a considerable quantity was going waste. In this regard, a public petition was filed and the Honbl'e High court ordered sealing the outlet of certain lakes. The closing of tank-outlets as directed by the Hon'ble High Court resulted in copious storage of water in most of the lakes and also significant improvement in underground water table. The farmers who had installed bore wells were able get more water and in turn increase their productivity, especially of those vegetables and flowers that required more water consumption. As a result, K.R Puram market saw larger quantities of goods coming for trading for several years. This led to more people from the labour classes turning into street vendors. Presently, about 12,000 people are dependent on this market—directly or indirectly for their livelihood. Among them, about 150–200 households are indirectly dependent on this market. These are the people who own transportation vehicles that carry vegetables and fruits from farmlands to the market.

The rise of IT industry and a few educational institutions in close proximity to this market in the recent past has led to more and more people coming here for buying their requirements.. According to information from the trading community, the volume of trading which was about Rs. 8 to 10 lakhs per day in the last decade has increased to about Rs. 30 to 35 lakhs per day. This phenomenal increase is attributed to the IT companies and a sizeable number of residential apartments that came up in recent times in close proximity to the market.

Some of these features make this market an interesting case to study.

5.2.3 Jayanagar Market

Jayanagar is one of the most sought after residential locality in Bengaluru with its greeneries and parks. The Jayanagar market, though does not look modern (see Fig. 5.3), continues to be one of the bustling market places in the city. Built in 1976, the present shopping complex is located in the centre of Jayanagar in the 4th Block. The Bengaluru Metropolitan Transport Corporation (BMTC) Transit Point is also nearby. The shopping complex is on a 15,000 m^2 plot, and has shops of all kinds in it; these include retail shops, vegetable market, wholesale yard, fish market, banks, Government offices etc.

5.3 A Brief Note on Markets from Tumkur

Tumkur is one of the middle performing districts (in terms of income) of Karnataka, which is around 70 km from Bengaluru, the state capital. The district of Tumkur is around 10597 km^2 and comprises 10 taluks (district sub divisions), namely, Tumkur, Koratagere, Sira, Gubbi, Pavagada, Turuvekere, Kunigal, Madhugiri, Tiptur and Chikkanayakanahalli. As per 2011 India census, Tumkur has a population of 305,821 with a density of 243 person per km^2. The average literacy rate of Tumkur district is 75%, which is higher than the national average of 59.5% with male literacy at 79%, and female literacy at 70%.

Economy and Industrial Profile:

This agrarian district is known for the traditional paddy and ragi cultivation and commercial crops like groundnut. Other commonly cultivated crops in the district are millet, rice, pulses, areca nut and oil seeds. It has a few industries like making of coarse cotton cloths, woollen blankets, ropes and watches. Iron ore is mined in large quantities from the hillsides while excellent building-stone is obtained from its quarries. The district is known for its mineral wealth - magnesite, granite, dolomite, iron ore, limestone, manganese and Soapstone. The iron ore mined acts as a major raw material for steel and other industries in the district as well the State.

Fig. 5.3 Jayanagar market. Photos taken by the authors

Jayanagar Market Location Map – Local Target respondents

Source for the map:www.google.co.in/maps

Fig. 5.3 (continued)

5.3.1 Vinayaka Market

Tumkur city has a couple of commercial markets dealing with fruits and vegetables, utensils, clothes and grocery related items (see Fig. 5.4). The Market referred as "Vinayaka Market" is exclusively meant for fruits and vegetables, and the oldest market in the city. The market is situated at the centre of the City on J C Road in close proximity to the regional transport bus stand. This market comprises of about 220 regular shops and another 250 street vendors operating in the market. The traders/vendors in the market consist of trader of all kinds and denominations: Hindu and Muslim, large and small, either with a shelter or sitting on the pavement, selling flower, vegetables etc. All these features make this another interesting case to study.

This market is well known for its weekly fair which is conducted on every Wednesday. More than 100 vendors earn their livelihood by selling flowers and vegetables at the market.

The market wakes up by as early as 5 AM., flowers and vegetables are delivered locally by farmers from adjoining villages of Tumkur city, while fruits are mainly sourced either from Bengaluru city or the adjoining districts. Apart from local consumption, vegetables and fruits are transported to neighbouring taluks in Tumkur district from this market. Customers of this market are largely from poor and lower middle class groups. The other bulk buyers who regularly visit the market are from the hotel industry that caters to the needs of Tumkur city.

Similarly, there are more than 50 shops exclusively dealing in utensils and plastic products situated on Mandipet road, close to the fruits and vegetables market (see map in Fig. 5.4). Shops selling clothes/chappals/Fancy items, etc. are situated on M G Road, parallel to vegetable/fruits and utensils market. This is the only

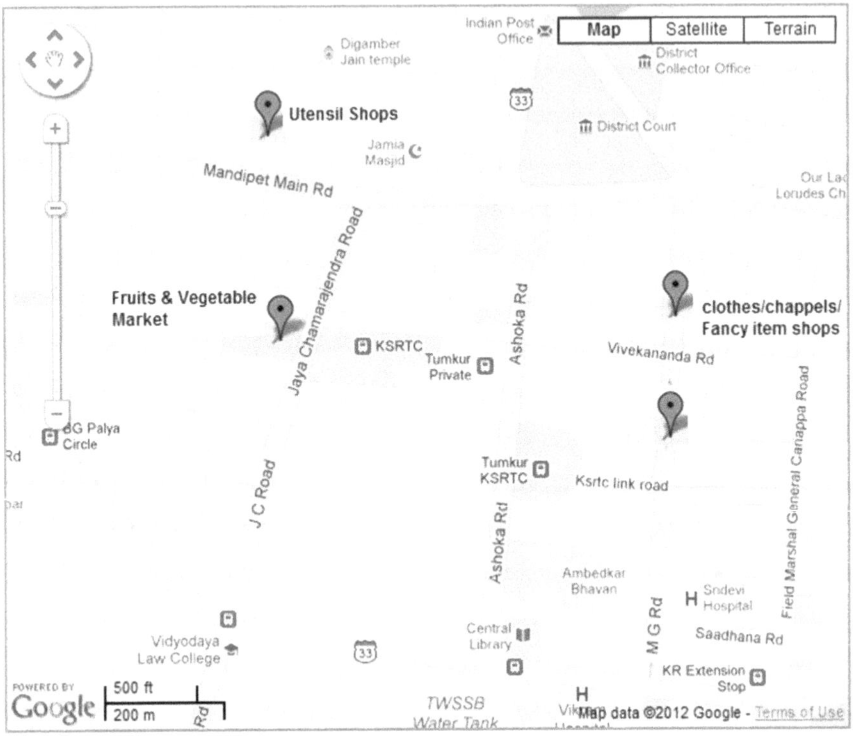

Source for the map:www.google.co.in/maps

Fig. 5.4 Tumkur city map—location of target respondents

street in this locality where the above mentioned goods are sold, and a sizeable number of shops (approximately 150–200) operate on this street. Interestingly, majority of them are into similar kind of trade—dealing with clothes/shoes and fancy items. Needless to say this is one the busiest markets for clothes and fancy items in Tumkur city.

5.3.2 Gubbi Town Market

Gubbi is one of the Taluks of Tumkur district and Gubbi town[2] is the taluk head-quarter of Gubbi Taluk. It is located on National Highway 206 and is about 90 km from Bengaluru city. Local markets for cotton and areca nut of this region were historically famous. As early as in 1871, Gubbi town had become a municipality.

[2]Source: http://en.wikipedia.org/wiki/Gubbi.

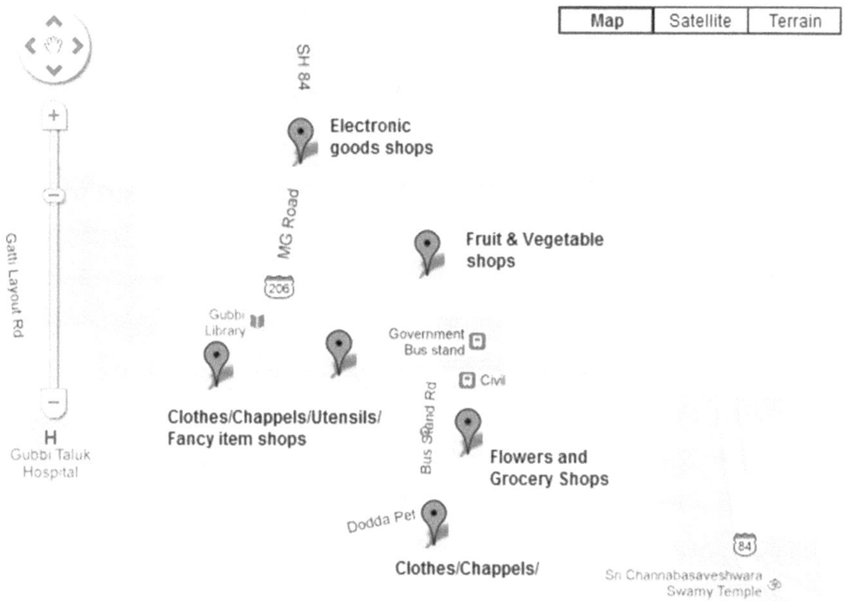

Source for the map:www.google.co.in/maps

Fig. 5.5 Gubbi town map—location of target respondents

Gubbi, though being the taluk headquarter, less energetic place in terms of business activities. As such there is no concept of a separate market[3] for fruit and vegetables except a big state run Agriculture Product Marketing Corporation (APMC) yard situated opposite to Bus stand. Two streets running perpendicular to each other constitute the hub for the entire business activities of the town (see Fig. 5.5). Thus this market we consider would give us a slightly different perspective compared to the more bustling markets.

A survey was conducted in these selected markets of the two districts using structured questionnaires which were personally canvassed. Some of the findings from the survey are discussed in the following chapters.

[3]Recently, the municipality has built a small size market which is able to accommodate about 25 shops and requested small vegetable vendors to operate from these shops. However, it emerged from our interaction that the street vendors are reluctant to shift as it would affect their business. As a result, these shops have remained unoccupied.

Chapter 6
Sample Characteristics: Markets Located in Bengaluru and Tumkur

The purpose of this Chapter is to understand the essential characteristics of the population engaged in the trading activities in our sample region to provide a background for the subsequent discussion of financial exclusion. Two of the most important indicators we are concerned with are level of income and education. Our analysis of NSSO data reveals that income is a critical indicator for financial inclusion. Information regarding education is not available from NSSO sources (of 59th or 70th rounds) but we believe education too is crucial given the fact that formal banking procedures are much more complex than that of informal institutions.

As discussed in the previous chapter, a sample of 300 small traders are selected from Bengaluru Urban district, operating in 3 major markets viz., the City Market, Jayanagar and the K R Puram markets; general characteristics of the markets are delineated above. Before moving on to the primary question on financial exclusion it is necessary to have an idea about some of the general attributes of the respondents as this will help to highlight the characteristics of the individuals who face exclusion. To begin with, let us concentrate on markets situated in Bengaluru. With age, overall human experience increases and this may in turn impact one's attitude towards financial intermediaries. As low as 2% of our respondents are below 25 years of age while as high as 36% are above 46 years, and the rest falls in the in between age group (Table A6.1 in the Appendix), leaving a large proportion of respondents in middle aged group. As far as their experience in business is concerned some of the traders we interviewed had established shops prior to 1980, but a large number of shops are of post 1995 origin (Table A6.1). We also hypothesize that size and the type of business one is engaged in would have a direct bearing on her/his level of access to financial services. In this respect our focus is on the small traders and most of the respondents included in our sample are either vendors of fruits, vegetables and flowers (39%) or low cost consumer goods (41%). Only 4% of the traders in our sample deal with moderately expensive consumer durables like electronic good (Table A6.2 in the Appendix). Importantly, our survey revealed certain difference in attitude towards formal banks between male and female respondents (10% of our respondents are women) (Table A6.1). Thirty percent of our respondents belong to Muslim community, and in certain areas Muslims have associations that provide financial services to community members (Table A6.1).

M. Rajeev and B.P. Vani, *Financial Access of the Urban Poor in India*,
SpringerBriefs in Economics, DOI 10.1007/978-81-322-3712-9_6

Table 6.1 Investment, Turnover and Profit (in Rs): Classification made according to type of business, Bengaluru

Type of Business	Amount (in Rs.) Invested at the time of Establishment			Daily turnover of the traders		Daily profit of the traders	
				Non festive season		Non festive season	
	Mean	Median	CV	Mean	Median	Mean	Median
Vegetables or fruits	5001	4000	106	6884	5000	874	850
Flower vendors	6308	1250	223	2682	1500	495	475
Consumer goods of daily use	31,181	9000	446	2828	1800	549	500
Consumer durables (electronics and Others)	175,333	20,000	160	2025	2000	806	875
Eatery/tea vendor/others	9000	9000	47	850	850	300	300
Total	20,983	5000	489	4507	2500	686	563

Source Field survey

As mentioned, access to education and economic status indeed help directly as well as indirectly in accessing formal financial institutions. Ironically, about 1/3rd of the respondent in our sample are illiterates; another 40% have had primary education only and about 4% are graduates (Table A6.1). Income of the respondents are analysed separately (see Table 6.1) but data on indirect indicators on economic status reveals that about 70% of them live in rented house (see Table A6.1) and television is the notable consumer durable every household owns, followed by vehicles—mainly two wheelers—owned by about 45% households (see Table A6.1). Presumably, they have started business with very little investment—mostly below Rs. 20,000—but the modal value shown is between Rs 1001 and Rs 5000 (Table A6.1). This is also corroborated by the fact that only 21 percent of the respondents have their own space/establishment in the market; the rest sit in open space or use handcart (Table A6.1).

As can be seen from Table 6.1, traders who deal with consumer durables like music player, TV or mobile phones, mainly of local brands, have the highest amount of investment, followed by traders of consumer goods of daily use like clothing, shoes etc. (Table 6.1).[1]

It is however interesting to note that with very low investment vegetable traders enjoy a reasonably high turnover, while turnover of the traders dealing with consumer durables is much lower (Table 6.1); yet the profit margins are comparatively high for them (Table 6.1). Expectedly, total profit of the vegetable traders remains

[1]There are of course traders with higher level of investment in the same market area, operating bigger shops. Our discussions with these traders reveal that they are utilizing the banking services fully.

Table 6.2 Total family income (in Rs. per month) of the traders classified according to type of business, Bengaluru (figures shown are percentages of traders)

Type of Business	Family income classes					
	< = 5000	5001–10,000	10,001–15,000	15,001–25,000	> = 25,001	Total
Vegetables or fruits	1.8	10.7	26.8	32.1	28.6	100.0
Flower vendors	7.1	14.3	28.6	50.0		100.0
Consumer goods of daily use	–	–	35.8	47.2	17.0	100.0
Consumer durables (electronics and others)	–	–	–	50.0	50.0	100.0
Eatery/tea vendor/others			100.0			100.0
Total	1.6	6.3	30.5	40.6	21.1	100.0

Source Field survey

Table 6.3 Per day expenditure of a street vendor in City Market, Bengaluru

Street vendors on peripheral area of City Market complex		Vendors operating from inside market complex (but not from regular shops)
Bribe to different officials (3 persons @ Rs. 20 each) per day	Rs. 60/-	Rs. 60/-
To Police (2 person @ Rs. 20 each) per day	Rs. 40/-	Rs. 40/-
Bribe/charge to shop owners	–	Rs. 100/-
Total	Rs. 100/-	Rs. 200/-

Source Field survey

high owing to substantially high turnover level; besides, vegetable traders sit mostly in the open space paying comparatively low ground-fee for the space occupied by them. Another interesting and significant observation from survey is that the persons who are engaged in consumer durables have much higher family income presumably because there are other members in the family who earn (Table 6.2) regular income. It is important to note that there is considerable difference between festive and non festive season income where the traders have much higher level of income during the festive season as shown in Table A6.2 in the Appendix.

In this context, it is of interest to highlight some of the costs incurred by the traders operating in the market. These estimates are based on inputs from City Market, Bengaluru. A person operating outside the proper market complex, for example, on pavements etc., has to pay bribe to various entities, while traders who sit inside the market complex usually in front of a regular shop pay a rent of Rs. 100 per day rent to the shop owner who allows him to carry out his business (perhaps not legally) in that space (see Table 6.3).

Thus one of the important observations from the survey is that a large number of self employed respondents earn reasonably high incomes of over Rs. 15,000 per month, and therefore have sufficient financial resources to avail the services of a financial intermediaries for various purposes including savings and investment.

Let us now discuss some of our findings from Tumkur, from where we have collected 200 sample observations. With age, experience of a trader increases, and this may in turn impact ones attitude towards financial intermediary. In the Tumkur sample, the age distribution of respondent traders is found to be similar to that of Bengaluru, but participation of relatively older persons is observed to be higher in Tumkur than in Bengaluru. About 1.3% of our respondents are below 25 years of age, about 40% above 46 years, and the rests fall in the in—between age group (Table A6.3 in the Appendix). Secondly the size and type of business also can impact ones access to financial resources. Therefore our focus is on the small traders where most of the respondents included in our sample were either vendors of fruits and vegetables (39%) or low cost consumer goods (45%). (Table A6.4 in the Appendix). Only 16% of traders in our sample deal with moderately expensive consumer durables like electronic good (Table A6.4). Access to education indeed helps in accessing formal financial institutions. In our sample about 20% of the respondent traders are illiterates, while another 36% have had only primary education and about 5% are graduates (Table A6.3). Thus levels of education of the Tumkur traders are marginally better than that of Bengaluru traders. As far as wealth related indicators are concerned we observed that percentage of respondents residing in their own houses also are much higher in Tumkur, at 53% (see Table A6.3), where television is the consumer durable everybody owns, vehicles—mainly two-wheelers—being the other commonly owned consumer durable (37%), (see Table A6.3).

Capital investment of certain groups (vegetable traders and consumer durables of daily use) in Tumkur markets is found higher than that of similar groups in Bengaluru (Table 6.4). About 60% of the respondents have their own space/

Table 6.4 Investment, Turnover and Profit (in Rs): Classification made according to type of business, Tumkur

Type of business	Amount (in Rs.) invested at the time of establishment			Daily turnover of the traders		Daily profit of the traders	
				Non festive season		Non festive season	
	Mean	Median	CV	Mean	Median	Mean	Median
Vegetables or fruits	9257.6	3000	167.2	2803	2000	344	338
Flower vendors	2400.0	1000	100.3	694	788	163	163
Consumer goods of daily use	37,785.7	30,000	90.3	2295	2000	373	325
Consumer durables (electronics and others)	42,671.9	45,000	85.3	3066	3000	503	400
Others	2000.0	2000		500	500	150	150
Total	25,830.6	8000	122.5	2537	2125	375	350

Source Field survey

establishment in the market while the rest occupy open space or use handcart (Table A6.3).

Amongst the traders of Tumkur, vegetable traders enjoy comparatively higher turnover though their average turnover is found to be little lower than that of Bengaluru (Table 6.4). The business-volume (turn over) of Bengaluru flower vendors is markedly higher than that in Tumkur may be due to the fact that City Market in Bengaluru (which is our major sample market) is particularly famous for flower trading. Turnover of Tumkur traders of other consumer durables is comparable with Bengaluru traders (Table 6.4). Profit margin on the consumer durables (electronics goods) of higher value is higher in Tumkur too (Table 6.4); but as expected the overall Profit levels in Tumkur are somewhat lower than that in Bengaluru.

Over 80% of our respondent traders have monthly income of over Rs 10,000 (Table A6.3) which is quite high for a small town resident, and about 29 percent of traders have monthly income above Rs 15,000 while their income levels during the festive season are much higher. Though these traders are economically better off, their patronage of formal financial services is not seen to be very impressive and it was a felt need that the reasons for this phenomenon need to be probed. This leads us to the investigation of the level of financial exclusion and reasons behind such deprivations as presented in the next chapter.

Appendix

Table A6.1 Characteristics of respondents, Bengaluru

Characteristics		Percent
Gender	Male	90
	Female	10
	Total	100.0
Religion	Hindu	70
	Muslim	30
	Total	100.0
Age class interval	<25	2.3
	26–35	35.3
	36–45	26.3
	>46	36.1
	Total	100.0
Education Category	Illiterate	29.3
	Primary	39.8
	Secondary	26.3
	Graduate and above	4.5
	Total	100.0

(continued)

Table A6.1 (continued)

Characteristics		Percent
Ownership of house	Rent	64.7
	Own	29.3
	Lease	6.0
	Total	100.0
Asset owned	House	29.3
	Vehicle	45.9
	TV	96.2
	Fridge	9.0
	Total	100.0
Year of establishment of business	up to 1980	4.6
	up to 1990	13.1
	up to 1995	14.6
	up to 2000	20.8
	up to 2005	23.8
	after 2005	23.1
	Total	100.0
Amount invested at the time of establishment	Up to Rs. 1000	18.3
	Rs. 1001–5000	33.0
	Rs. 5001–10,000	25.2
	Rs. 10,001–20,000	15.7
	Rs. 20,001–50,000	5.2
	Rs. 50,001 and above	2.6
	Total	100.0
Space availability for running business	Street vendor-open space	67.67
	Regular shop	21.05
	Pull cart	11.28
	Total	100.00
Total family income (monthly in Rs.)	< = 5000	1.6
	5001–10,000	6.3
	10,001–15,000	30.5
	15,001–25,000	40.6
	> = 25,001	21.1
	Total	100.0

Source Field survey

Table A6.2 Income of the respondents: Classification made according to type of business, Bengaluru

Type of Business	Percent	Daily turnover				Daily profit			
		Festive Season		Non Festive Season		Festive Season		Non Festive Season	
		Mean	Median	Mean	Median	Mean	Median	Mean	Median
Vegetables or fruits	43.6	13,454	8500	6884	5000	1671	1500	874	850
Flower vendors	10.5	4850	2500	2682	1500	825	750	495	475
Consumer goods of daily use	41.4	4704	3500	2828	1800	922	900	549	500
Consumer durables (electronics and others)	3.0	2975	3000	2025	2000	1250	1200	806	875
Eatery/ tea vendor/ others	1.5	1100	1100	850	850	550	550	300	300
Total	100.0	8387	4500	4507	2500	1239	1000	686	563

Source Field survey

Table A6.3 Characteristics of respondents, Tumkur

Characteristics		Percent
Gender	Male	79
	Female	21
	Total	100
Religion	Hindu	64
	Muslim	36
	Total	100
Age class interval	<25	1.3
	26–35	22.4
	36–45	36.8
	>46	39.5
	Total	100.0
Education category	Illiterate	20.0
	Primary	36.0
	Secondary	38.7
	Graduate and above	5.3
	Total	100.0
Ownership of house	Rent	46.1
	Own	52.6
	Lease	1.3
	Total	100.0

(continued)

Table A6.3 (continued)

Characteristics		Percent
Asset owned	House	30.1
	Vehicle	37.0
	TV	98.6
	Fridge	5.5
	Total	100.0
Space availability for running business	Street vendor-open space	40.5
	Regular shop	59.5
	Pull cart	–
	Total	100.00
Total family income (monthly in Rs.)	< = 5000	9.9
	5001–10,000	4.4
	10,001–15,000	57.1
	15,001–25,000	24.2
	> = 25,001	4.4
	Total	100.0

Source Field survey

Table A6.4 Type of business of respondents, Tumkur

Type of Business	Percent
Vegetables or fruits	36
Flower vendors	3
Consumer goods of daily use	45
Consumer durables (electronics and others)	16
Eatery/tea vendor/others	–
Total	100.0

Source Field survey

Chapter 7
Understanding the Nature of Financial Exclusion: Experiences from Field Survey in Bengaluru and Tumkur

7.1 Introduction

The previous chapter delineates the basic characteristics of our respondents (sample group), who are primarily self-employed in trading business and in regular need of funds, in particular, for meeting their working capital. A few characteristics came out striking. The First concerns the respondents' income level which appears to be quite high, and comparable with the income of any middle class salaried person. In contrast however, their level of education is much lower as one-third of the respondents are illiterates and another 40% have had only primary education. Thus around 75% of the respondent traders have primary education or below. In contrast, among the salaried class one would find much more people with graduation or above level of education. Thirdly, most respondents seem to have not been able to acquire consumer durables or other property despite their reasonably satisfactory income probably due to lack of access to credit facility.

Objective of this chapter is to study the level of financial inclusion of the respondents and classify them on the basis of their degree of financial inclusion. This exercise will help us to estimate the respective percent of respondents who are either fully or partially excluded from formal financial services. This, in turn will provide insights into the extent of the problem, in particular, where the agents have the option to visit several banks located within a radius of around1 km from their place of business. Secondly, such a classification would aid us to identify the correlation between extent of exclusion and other characteristics of the respondents. We also then identify the reasons for exclusion through our survey to arrive at appropriate policy prescriptions.

M. Rajeev and B.P. Vani, *Financial Access of the Urban Poor in India*,
SpringerBriefs in Economics, DOI 10.1007/978-81-322-3712-9_7

7.2 Experiences from Bengaluru

7.2.1 Sources of Funds for Income Generating Activities

As most of these traders are street vendors, their initial investments are modest; ranging mostly between Rs. 5000–10,000, and sourced primarily from one's own savings (see Col. 4, Table 7.1). However, even for the traders dealing in consumer durables where the initial investment required is substantially higher, one's own savings seem to be the sole source of finance. This indirectly indicates that a person starts business on a scale commensurate with his/her own savings and investment funding through credit is almost nil.

More importantly none of these traders, large or small, irrespective of the goods they intended to deal in seem to have approached formal banks for credit for their initial business investment.

Terms and Conditions of working capital loan: Insights from Field

We next examine the working capital needs of the traders. As can be seen from Table 7.2, over 50% of the requirement comes from credit. Here, the sources of credit are mainly wholesalers from whom the retail traders get goods on credit basis. Repayment of credit is generally after selling the goods taken on credit. Credit is usually given for a period of 15 days to one month, depending on the kind of goods involved. For instance, vegetables and fruit traders get credit for 15 days while the traders of consumer goods of daily use such as clothes get up to one month to repay. Regarding the terms and conditions, it is seen that there is no cash benefit from wholesale traders with respect to fruits, vegetables and flowers in all sample markets. In essence, goods purchased through credit are not entitled for any higher price tag. On the other hand, non-food consumer goods such as clothes and other items are entitled for certain discount. In cash purchase transaction, the retailer is entitled to a discount of Rs. 10/- (for each piece of readymade garment). Terms and conditions of private money lenders are presented in Table 7.3.

From Table 7.2, we can infer that while a trader accesses credit facility on a regular basis for working capital needs, they hardly avail formal sources of funds. Indeed the new businesses entail much adverse terms and conditions resulted in much lower savings for the retailer which in turn makes the borrower perpetually dependent on credit. *Thus, there is a necessity to target this group of budding business enterprises.*

Given that these business enterprises have generally remained outside the ambit or being forced out of, the formal financial network, it is of interest to examine the level of their exclusion. Such an exercise is particularly useful to unravel the reasons for exclusion despite their apparent easy physical access to banks (spatially) and possessing sufficient financial resources.

Table 7.1 Initial investment and sources of funds, Bengaluru

Col. 1	Col. 2	Col. 3	Col. 4	Sources of loan (amount in Rs.)					
Type of business	Average total amount of initial investment in Rs.	Out of amount shown in Col. 2		Out of the amount shown in Col. 3 amount of loan obtained from (average)					
		Average amount of loan taken in Rs.	Average amount of own funds used in Rs.	Bank	Trader/whole seller	Money lender	Relatives	Friends	Others
Vegetables or fruits	5001	510 (10.2%)	4491 (89.8%)	0	0	0	163 (3.3%)	41 (0.8%)	306 (6.1%)
Flower vendors	6308	208 (3.3%)	6100 (96.7%)	0	0	0	208 (3.3%)	0	0
Consumer goods of daily use	31,181	2605 (8.3%)	28,576 (91.6%)	0	0	1078 (3.5%)	1139 (3.7%)	328 (1.1%)	59 (0.2%)
Consumer durables (electronics and others)	1,75,333	2333 (1.3%)	1,73,000 (98.7%)	0	0	0	2333 (1.3%)	0	0
Eatery/tea vendor/others	9000	500 (5.6%)	8500 (94.4%)	0	0	0	500 (5.6%)	0	0
Total	20,983	1439 (6.9%)	19,544 (93.1%)	0	0	470 (2.2%)	655 (3.1%)	160 (0.8%)	154 (0.7%)

Source Field survey

Note Figures in bracket are shares of credit obtained from different sources to total. For example, out of the total funds invested by vegetable traders, 10.2% are through loans and 3.3% of the total loan amount is from relatives etc. Average loan figures are rather low as many traders have not borrowed and when averaged out borrowing amount turned out to be miniscule

Table 7.2 Working capital needs and sources of funds, Bengaluru

Col. 1	Col. 2	Col. 3	Col. 4	Sources of credit (amount in Rs.)					
Type of business	Average total amount of working capital requirement in Rs.	Out of amount shown in Col. 2		Out of the credit shown in Col. 3 amount of credit obtained from					
		Average credit requirement	Own amount (in Rs.)	Bank	Trader/ wholesaler	Money lender	Relatives	Friends	Others
Vegetables or fruits	24,885	8521 (34.2%)	16,363 (65.8%)	0	8218 (33.0%)	182 (0.7%)	91 (0.4%)	13 (5.5%)	18 (0.07%)
Flower vendors	12,050	7089 (58.8%)	4961 (41.2%)	0	5304 (44.0%)	1429 (11.9%)	357 (3.0%)	0	0
Consumer goods of daily use	27,113	17,376 (64.1%)	9737 (35.9%)	0	17,093 (63.0%)	283 (1.0%)	0	0	0
Consumer durables (electronics and others)	36,875	22,500 (61.0%)	14,375 (39.0%)	0	22,500 (61.0%)	0	0	0	0
Eatery/tea vendor/ others	1000	0	1000 (100.0%)	0	0	0	0	0	0
Total	24,405	12,335 (50.5%)	12,071 (49.5%)	0	11,892 (48.7%)	352 (1.4%)	78 (0.3%)	5 (0.02%)	8 (0.03%)

Source Field survey
Note Figures in the bracket are share of credit obtained from different sources to total. For example, out of the total average credit requirement vegetable business 33.0% are through wholesale traders. 0.7% of the total credit requirement is from Money lenders etc.

Table 7.3 Terms and conditions of private money lenders: K.R. market, Bengaluru

Type of vendors/ trader	Principal amount (for every)	Actual amount received	Nature of repayment	Amount to be paid	No. of days	Total repayment amount
New or startup	Rs. 10,000	Rs. 8000	Daily	Rs. 100	100	Rs. 10,000
Regular/ old/loyal	Rs. 10,000	Rs. 9000	Daily	Rs. 100	100	Rs. 10,000
	Rs. 10,000	Rs. 9000	Weekly	Rs. 1000	10 week	Rs. 10,000
	Rs. 10,000	Rs. 9300	Daily	Rs. 100	100	Rs. 10,000

Source Field survey

7.2.2 Measuring Financial Exclusion

In this backdrop it is necessary to rigorously evaluate the level and extent of financial exclusion for such an important group. Through this, we can also infer about the level of exclusion for other groups that are self employed in various different activities and may be less endowed (in this context Thorat (2007) talks about exclusion of slum dwellers).

Most of our respondents reported as having not obtained loan from banks for business purposes; however, a selected few have accessed bank for loans for consumer durables and a few among them also maintain credit cards. Keeping these characteristics of the sample group in view, we have assigned certain scores to the respondents based on the degree to which they have accessed selected services, as well as the relative importance of the services so accessed. While the scores look adhoc in some sense, only their relative ranking matters in arriving at the classification of the respondents as per their level of financial inclusion. In other words, the scoring pattern is ordinal in nature rather than cardinal. Secondly, given the abysmally low level of financial inclusion in the area of survey, a more elaborate classification in our view would not elicit any further insight.

Scoring pattern:

- Traders having current account/taken loan for trade purpose are assigned a score of 10 points.
- Loans taken for other consumption purposes from bank like vehicle loan, housing loan, education loan etc. get a score of 8 points.
- Possessing savings account and operating regularly (once in 3 months): 6 points
- Family members having an account: 4 points
- Using banking services occasionally (once a year or so) for other purpose like term deposit/remittances etc. get a score of 2 points.
- Zero otherwise

After assigning scores, for each respondent for each of such activities, sum of the scores is obtained and on the basis of the final score so obtained by a trader he or she is classified as

- Included if points obtained are above 10
- Marginally excluded if the total score is between 8 and 10
- Severely excluded if score sum is between 2–6
- Fully excluded when the sum is zero.

Given this scoring pattern, Table A7.1 in the Appendix shows the distribution of respondents according to their level of financial exclusion. Here we observe that as high as 44% of these self employed agents/respondents (having banking facility in the neighbourhood) are not using the facility for any purposes at all. We note that this percentage compares well with the level of exclusion seen in the rural regions (before the financial inclusion drive in the state). (Some estimates claim that about 67% of urban population is financial included (see Chakrabarty 2013). But if we consider the less educated population in urban regions this seems to be an over estimate both from our survey and NSSO data).

In the absence of data on urban financial exclusion Table A7.1 itself is revealing as the table displays certain interesting features. First, about 45% of the respondents have no linkage with the formal banking system. Another 34% are severely excluded meaning not having even a savings account, and may have visited bank once or twice in their lifetime for certain occasional requirements. Thus about 80% of these self employed persons do not experience any meaningful financial inclusion. Certain other characteristics of this group also need to be highlighted. First, this is a group with substantial regular flow of income and needs credit on a regular basis. Secondly, formal financial institutions are numerous in their neighbourhood. These are some of the unique features of urban financial exclusion so far not discussed much in the literature (the most recent scenario is also approximately the same as discussed in the sequel).

7.2.3 Associations with Other Characteristics of the Traders

While the above exercise that throws light on the access to financial services itself is enlightening, especially in the light of the cash transfer policy adopted by the Government, as a next step, it is necessary to relate this state to various characteristics of the respondents as it will help to identify the causes of exclusion. Thus, having classified the agents with respect to their level of exclusion, we next examine using chi-square statistics, the level of association between exclusion and other indicators relating to the respondents. First, we wish to highlight that the levels of education plays a crucial role in financial inclusion. As can be seen from Table A7.2 in the Appendix, while only 2% of illiterates are found to have high level of financial inclusion, this percentage is as high as 50% for the graduates.

Ironically however about 50% of the graduate self employed are almost or fully excluded. But as the level of education declines, degree of financial exclusion increases (see the last column of Table A7.2). Statistical tests have shown a significant association between the variables indicating that as the level of education increases, extent of financial inclusion also increases.

Secondly, significant association is also found between the types of business and the level of exclusion/inclusion. As can be seen from Table A7.2, none of the respondents who deal in consumer durables and electronic goods are fully excluded financially. It is in contrast with the high level of exclusion seen for flower vendors (64.3%), followed by tea vendors (50%) and vegetable and fruit sellers (46.6%). Table A7.2 reveals two additional interesting facts. Our analysis in the previous chapter has shown that traders dealing in consumer durables have made the highest level of initial investment. Thus higher initial investment, coming from higher level of household savings is seen to be associated with better financial inclusion. Secondly, most of the flower vendors are women and the lowest level of inclusion of this group also reveals a gender angle to the problem. More importantly, direct association is seen between economic status of the respondent and his/her level of financial inclusion, which is on expected lines. Here, economic status is measured in terms of monthly profit earned by the respondent as well as the total family income. Both these exercises show that higher economic status is indicative of better inclusion (chi-square values are significant) (see Table A7.2). Finally, we consider two other indicators viz., age of the trader as it represents level of experience and the type of shelter for business (having a regular shop or not). Both these variables show lack of association (chi-square value not being significant) (see Table A7.2). Thus, the assertion of the respondents that due to their not having proper shop address, banks are reluctant to give loan and as a result they did not approach banks is not found to be true. It is found that even the traders with regular shops have not been approaching banks for various other reasons as discussed below.

7.2.4 Understanding Determinants of Exclusion: A Comprehensive Analysis

Though the above analysis provides useful insights and explains the link between financial inclusion and other characteristics of a trader, it explains association between two indicators only. To understand the influence of different variables on financial exclusion, we have devised an ordered logistic regression model where the dependent variable is the above mentioned exclusion index. As can be seen from Table 7.4 income is a significant determinant of financial exclusion – higher the level of income lower the level of exclusion and similar is the result with regard to the level of education. Chances of being financially excluded are inversely related to the level of education, i.e., as the level of education goes up,

Table 7.4 Ordered logistic regression: understanding determinants of exclusion, Bengaluru

Wald Chi2 = 39.15		Prob > Chi2 = 0.000		
Log Pseudolikelihood = −131.67		Pseudo R2 = 0.2414		
Variable	Coeff	Robust std_err	Z	P > |Z|
age_yng	0.2098	0.5095	0.41	0.681
old_est	−0.1384	0.5109	−0.27	0.786
income	−0.0001*	0.0000	−3.20	0.001
edu_pri (primary education)	−0.4268	0.4982	−0.86	0.392
edu_sec (secondary education)	−1.5319*	0.5175	−2.96	0.003
veg_fru (vegetable and fruit traders)	1.5489***	0.8966	1.73	0.084
con_good (light consumer goods)	1.4435***	0.8753	1.65	0.099
flower	2.1986**	0.9537	2.31	0.021
reg_shop	−0.1902	0.4380	−0.43	0.664
/cut1	−4.1857	1.2201		
/cut2	−2.9143	1.2001		
/cut3	−0.9174	1.1220		

Note Dependent variable: Level of Financial exclusion defined as
Highly Included = 1, Marginally Excluded = 2, Severely Excluded = 3, Fully Excluded = 4
Education Illiterates constitute the base category; Type of business: Consumer durables, electronic goods is base category; age_yng are those traders who are less than 35 years of age and old_est are the establishments came up prior to 2000; reg_shop: those who own regular shop
*1% level of sig., **5% level of sig., ***10% level of sig

chances of financial exclusion declines. However, there does not seem to be significant difference between illiterates and those with primary education in regard to financial exclusion. *Thus there appears to be a threshold level for accessing formal banks where secondary to higher level of education is necessary*. Similarly traders dealing in light consumer durables (of daily use like clothing) and electronic goods are found to have lower level of exclusion compared to the other categories. Age does not appear to matter and so is the kind of shelter (regular shop, pavement or other unstructured shelters).

Thus as mentioned above the assertion that due to their not having a proper business shelter (address) they could not approach bank, is not found true.

7.2.5 *Reasons for not Approaching Formal Banks and Views of Banks*

The primary reason for not approaching a formal bank for initial capital was antipathy towards the formal banking system and the perception that bank procedures are cumbersome and not friendly to the small borrowers who do not own a shop or have any property as a form of security. Often this antipathy is not based on any hard evidence or experiences but seems to be herd behaviour.

More precisely, about 80% of the respondents have a rather pessimistic attitude towards banking sector. The respondents primarily financed their investment through their own savings and a small percentage of them (25%) borrowed partly from private money lenders. About 7% of the borrowers responded that their business falls in negative list of banks and hence it is not possible to get formal credit.

While most traders have managed initial investment through own savings, for working capital needs all most all of these self employed persons depend on credit. Credit is obtained primarily from the whole seller (80%) and the rest (20%) managed through funds obtained from their daily sales. Interestingly only 18% of our respondents reported as having approached banks but got rejected due to reasons such as not having asset, lack of proper project documentation or not fulfilling certain regulations. But, as high as 88% of the respondents have a negative attitude towards bank, though without any personal negative experience, out of which 52% felt that bank procedures are too complicated for small borrowers like them.

Views of Banks

The above discussions show that the self employed persons in our sample did not accessed bank facilities for credit for their business activities primarily due to perceived inapproachability of the banking sector. To get a balanced view, we also held discussions with selected bank officials in the city of Bengaluru in order to understand their perception of the problem. Some of the issues and suggestions put forward by the banks are reported below.

Crowding out effect: Firstly, the officials agree with the fact that the small vendors may find bank inapproachable, more so in urban areas primarily because banks in urban regions cater to a large number of middle and high income customers having good educational background as well as financial literacy. Therefore the street vendors and small traders usually get crowded out.

Transaction cost: Secondly, the office-timings of nationalized banks are not street vendor friendly, i.e., the rigid business hours of nationalized banks are not convenient to self employed persons who run their business without any additional supporting hands. As the opportunity cost of time during working hours of a bank is rather high for these persons, they avoid visiting banks. Private money lenders, on the other hand, visit them at their door step, usually in the early hours of the day or at the convenience of the borrowers.

Procedural problems: Small vendors often find 'know your customer norms' and other procedural problems difficult to handle due to their low level of education and knowledge.

7.3 Experiences from Tumkur

The situation in Tumkur is identical to that of Bengaluru in many ways. Most of the traders from Tumkur are street vendors, their initial investments are modest, ranging mostly between Rs. 5000–10,000 and this amount primarily comes from their own savings (see Col. 4, Table 7.5). But even for the traders dealing in consumer durables where initial investment is not small, sources of funds are generally from one's own savings. This indirectly indicates that a person's investment in business is limited to his/her own savings level, a fact which indirectly imply that it is impossible for persons without own funds to start any business activity to earn a living.

More importantly, none of these traders, large or small, irrespective of the type of goods they deal in seems to have approached formal banks for credit for their initial business investment.

We next examine the working capital needs of the traders. As can be seen from Table 7.6, about 60% of fund requirement comes from credit. The main source of credit is wholesale traders from whom the retail traders get goods on a credit, repayment of which is made after sale of the above goods. Credit is usually given for a period of 15 days to one month, depending on the kind of goods involved.

Table 7.5 Initial investment and sources of funds, Tumkur

Col. 1	Col. 2	Col. 3	Col. 4	Col. 5: Sources of loan (amount in Rs.)				
Type of business	Average amount of initial investment required	Out of amount shown in Col. 2		Out of the amount shown in Col. 3 amount of loan obtained from				
		Average amount of credit required	Own amount	Bank	Whole saler or trader	Private money lender	Relatives	Friends
Vegetable or fruit vendors	9258	3061 (33.1%)	6197 (66.9%)	0	0	561 (6.1%)	2500 (27.0%)	0
Flower vendors	2400	200 (8.3%)	2200 (91.7%)	0	200 (8.3%)	0	0	0
Consumer goods/ services of daily use	37,786	5771 (15.3%)	32,015 (84.7%)	0	0	714 (1.9%)	5057 (13.4%)	0
Consumer durables (electronics and others)	42,672	3281 (7.7%)	39,391 (92.3%)	0	3125 (7.3%)	0	156 (0.4%)	0
Others	2000	2000 (100%)	0	0	0	2000 (100%)	0	0
Total	26,530	4183 (15.8%)	22,347 (84.2%)	0	567 (2.1%)	706 (2.7%)	2911 (11.0%)	0

Source Field Survey
Note Figures in bracket show the share of credit obtained from different sources to total. For example, out of the total funds invested by vegetable traders, 33.1% is through loans and 27.0% of such loans are from relatives etc. As for the amounts, since many vendors do not get any loan—the average figures under Col. 5 turned out to be low

Table 7.6 Working Capital needs and sources of funds, Tumkur

Col. 1	Col. 2	Col. 3	Col. 4	Sources of loan (amount in Rs.)				
Type of business	Average amount of working capital required (in Rs.)	Out of amount shown in Col. 2		Out of the amount shown in Col. 3 amount of loan obtained from				
		Average amount of credit required (in Rs.)	Own amount (in Rs.)	Bank	Trader/whole saler	Private money lender	Relatives	Friends
Vegetable or fruit vendors	15,505	7542 (48.6%)	7962 (51.4%)	2220 (14.3%)	5073 (32.7%)	250 (1.6%)	0	0
Flower vendors	6700	700 (10.4%)	6000 (89.6%)	0	700 (10.4%)	0	0	0
Consumer goods/ services of daily use	27,914	16,043 (57.5%)	11,808 (42.3%)	714 (12.6%)	15,329 (54.2%)	0	0	0
Consumer durables (electronics and others)	30,938	24,625 (79.6%)	6313 (20.4%)	0	24,625 (79.6%)	0	0	0
Others	500	0	500 (100%)	0	0	0	0	0
Total	22,418	13,421 (59.9%)	8997 (40.1%)	1092 (4.9%)	12,238 (54.3%)	92 (0.4%)	0	0

Source Field Survey

Note Figures in the bracket are share of credit obtained from different sources to total. For example, out of the total Average credit requirement vegetable business 32.7% are through wholesale traders. 1.6% of the total credit requirement is from Money lenders etc

A special feature in Tumkur is that due to the personal initiatives of certain Bank officials, several borrowers have been able to access banks for credit needs.

A commendable effort of a Bank Manager in loan distribution at Tumkur…

In the year 2006–07, UCO bank of Tumkur branch had distributed loans to flower and vegetable vendors operating inside Market (Vinayaka market). This could happen only due to initiative of the then Branch Manager who initiated lending facilities to the traders. As part of repayment process, he entrusted one of the staffs as field officer who visited the borrowers once in a week and collected a sum of Rs. 1000/- from these vendors (as done by the informal lenders). In the process, principle amount along with the interest got fully repaid in 13 months. The traders who availed this facility sincerely thank the bank manager as his services helped them to improve their business. Although more than 70% of them repaid the loans, about 20–25% are yet to repay the loan completely. Such acts of personal initiative taken for the poor are seen more in small towns and not much in Metros.

7.3.1 Reasons for not Approaching Formal Banks and Views of Banks

As in Bengaluru, the primary reason cited for not approaching a formal bank for Initial Capital by Tumkur traders was antipathy towards the formal banking system (see Table A7.5) particularly the perception that the bank procedures are cumbersome and not friendly to the small borrowers who do not own a shop or have any property for security. Therefore, traders decide the type and size of business depending upon their investible savings. Often this antipathy is not based on any hard evidence or experiences.

Strangely, almost every respondent has a rather pessimistic attitude towards banking sector. The respondents primarily financed their investment through their own savings and a small percentage of them borrowed partly from private money lenders. About 1% of the borrowers responded that their type of business falls in the negative list of banks and hence it is not possible to get formal credit.

While most traders managed initial investment through own savings, for working capital needs all most all of them were dependent on credit. About 20% of credit is generally obtained from the whole-seller and the rest 20% managed through funds obtained from their daily sales.

Respondents from Tumkur have naturally suggested simplification of documentation and dissemination of information as the major steps needed to make bank accessible to poor self employed populace (see Table A7.5).

7.3.2 Measuring Financial Exclusion

The method of measuring financial inclusion is as delineated above. It is to be observed that in Bengaluru 8% of the traders are fully included while this percentage is a little higher for Tumkur at 12%. This is where the personal initiatives of the bank officials are found to have played a constructive role.

7.3.3 Financial Inclusion: Association with Other Characteristics of the Traders

Having classified the agents with respect to their level of exclusion, we next examine using chi-square statistics the level of association between exclusion and other characteristics of the respondents. First, it needs to be highlighted that level of education plays one of the important roles in financial inclusion. Tests carried out to check this have shown significant association between the variables indicating that as level of education increases, extent of financial inclusion also increases.

Secondly, significant association is also found between the type of business and degree of financial inclusion. As can be seen from Table A7.4, a smaller percentage of the respondents dealing in consumer durables and electronic goods (22 and 37) are also fully excluded. It may be recalled that in Bengaluru, none of the respondents who deal in consumer durables are fully excluded. Though this is not the case for Tumkur, their percentage is relatively low. On the other hand, high level of exclusion is seen for flower vendors (100%) who are generally women and hence we observe an element of gender dimension also in this finding.

More importantly, association exists between economic status of the respondent and level of financial inclusion. However, there is a difference in the degree of association between Bengaluru and Tumkur: while individual profit does not show a significant association with level of financial exclusion in Tumkur, family income did show a positive and significant association. Based on this observation, it can be concluded that economic status does matter in determining financial inclusion (Table A7.4).

Finally, we consider two other indicators viz., age of the trader as it represents the level of experience and the type of premises used for business, i.e., whether having a regular shop or not. It is also seen that age doesn't have any significant association with financial inclusion (see Table A7.4)

However ownership of regular shops does show a positive association (Table A7.4) presumably because regular shop owners are also the ones with higher income level in Tumkur, which is not necessarily the case in Bengaluru. As mentioned earlier, some of these shop owners in Tumkur obtained bank credit through the initiative of the UCO bank manager as mentioned above. In the markets of Bengaluru such as city market, there are vendors who earn reasonably high income without a proper shed in the market. It is worth noting in this context that unlike in Bengaluru, Tumkur vendors reported that they need not pay any bribe to anybody to do business without having a proper shed.

7.3.4 Understanding Determinants of Exclusion: An Econometric Analysis

Though the above analysis provides useful insights and explains the association between financial inclusion and other characteristics of a trader, it confines to explaining the association between two indicators only. Therefore, in order to understand the influence of different variables on financial exclusion in a comprehensive manner, we have devised an ordered logistic model and the significant variables can be seen. As can be observed from Table 7.7, income is a significant

Table 7.7 Ordered logistic regression: Understanding determinants of exclusion, Tumkur

Wald Chi2 = 49.96		Prob > Chi2= 0.000		
Log Pseudolikelihood = −111.85		Pseudo R2 = 0.2386		
Variable	Coef.	Robust std. err.	z	P>|z|
age_yng	−0.844	0.464	−1.820	0.069
old_est	−1.717	0.451	−3.800	0.000
Income	0.000	0.000	−4.080	0.000
reg_shop	−1.087	0.656	−1.660	0.098
edu_pri (primary education)	1.447	0.784	0.570	0.568
edu_sec (secondary education)	−0.447	0.777	−0.580	0.565
edu_coll	−2.179	1.023	−2.130	0.033
veg_fru (vegetable and fruit traders)	−1.537	0.829	−1.850	0.064
Flower	1.542	0.754	2.050	0.041
con_good (consumer goods)	−0.648	0.527	−1.230	0.219
/cut1	−7.174	1.329		
/cut2	−6.124	1.295		
/cut3	−3.654	1.198		

Note Dependent variable: Level of Financial exclusion defined as
Highly Included = 1, Marginally Excluded = 2, Severely Excluded = 3, Fully Excluded = 4
Education Illiterates constitute the base category; Type of business: Consumer durables, electronic goods is base category; age_yng are those traders who are less than 35 years of age and old_est are the establishments came up prior to 2000; reg_shop: those who own regular shop
*1% level of sig., **5% level of sig., ***10% level of sig

determinant of financial exclusion: higher the level of income lower the level of exclusion and vice versa. A similar result is seen with regard to level of education; chances of being financially excluded lowers as one goes up in the educational ladder right from the base category of illiterates. Interestingly, the difference becomes apparent only at the college level of education. At secondary level, though financial exclusion shows reduction it is not statistically significant. Like in case of Bengaluru, there does not seem to be significant difference between illiterates and primary education holders. Similarly the traders selling consumer durables and electronic goods have lower level of exclusion compared to the other categories. Age and kind of business-premises (regular shop, pavement or other unstructured shelters) too seem to matter in Tumkur unlike in Bengaluru. This result could be because traders who were helped by bank officials to access loans are mostly those with regular shops, and also younger in age (below 40 years).

To sum up, it is clear from the above observations that both economic status and level of education especially at a higher level are critical variables in determining the level of financial exclusion.

Difference between small town and metropolitan operation

The above comparison of metros with small towns shows the major difference between small towns and metropolitan regions. While indicators of financial exclusion and its determinants in respect of both the regions show qualitatively similar features, it is often observed that in smaller regions, sometimes some committed bank officials do take special interest to bring closeness between the banks and the needy. Such trends are more common in rural regions. During the course of one of our earlier surveys relating SHGs, (see Rajeev et al. 2015) we witnessed how initiative of the banks officials did indeed help the poor and uneducated to get linked with the banks. In the metros however, due to the work pressure and impersonal work culture, such trends are very rare, if not totally absent.

7.4 Has the Scenario Changed in Recent Times?

During the period of our survey Jan Dhan Yojana was just initiated. But subsequently we have again made field visits to understand whether after the recent drive the scenario has changed for the urban self employed who are in the lower strata. We observe that many of these traders who are less educated and have smaller business are still without a bank account. Many though have opened a bank account it is primarily used for getting subsidy for the cooking gas connections. In the rural areas on the contrary Jan Dhan accounts are more in use due to the larger number of state programmes India has for the rural populace. Access to credit, which is the major focus of this research therefore seen no improvement. However, during our revisit we encounter a few relatively larger traders who have opened bank account under Jan Dhan Yojana initiated by Mr Modi's Government and subsequently have been able to access smaller size credit as well. Thus though we observe marginal improvement in financial inclusion, a lot remains to be done to make formal financial services accessible to the poorer sections in the urban regions of India.

7.5 Role of Business Correspondents (BC) or Facilitators

This study brings out how despite close physical proximity, indifference and apathy have created a void and resultant financial exclusion of the needy. The potential clients need the physical presence of financial intermediaries in their work premises so that they are easily accessible and willing to offer timely advice and support. This makes a strong case for stationing business correspondents in places where small traders run their business in the form of localised kiosks.

In 2006 the Reserve Bank of India issued new guidelines concerning business correspondents (BCs) and business facilitators[1] to enhance their outreach (see also Thorat 2010). Today we also have numerous technologies to carry out banking work through agents irrespective of spatial distance. Efforts under Jan Dhan Yojana are particularly worth mentioning. But it is quite clear that the BC model has not taken off substantially to make a real dent in the financial inclusion drive. Amongst other concerns, financial viability is an issue plaguing the BC operations in India. However, in the kind of spatial units that we focus here (such as urban market places) the traders seem to have substantial financial resources and also use the services of financial intermediaries on a regular basis; in such spatial units, the business volume of a BC can be large enough to give him or her a sustainable level of operation through both credit as well as savings facilities. For each such spatial unit, a maximum of two banks can post their BCs so that a viable economic proposition is ensured. A BC may need support and guidance from the respective bank for some time. Further, given the existence of formal banks in the vicinity the need for reporting to the banks on a regular basis is not an issue for the kind of population group we are concerned here. An already existing business enterprise preferably run by a large trader such as a grocery shop can act as a nodal centre and facilitators, or a BC. Such agents who already have long term relation with other agents in the locality and enjoy their good-will can help in building faith in the scheme. Thus building client confidence, meeting the exact needs of the clients, timely reporting to parent banks and adoption of simple and user-friendly

[1]Business Correspondents and Facilitators: Pathway to Financial Inclusion?: A Report of CAB, CGAP and Access, 2009.

technologies, are not insurmountable problems. The feasibility of such models can be explored in these spatial units to achieve financial inclusion of hitherto excluded sections. Experiences from other developing nations also can be quite useful for India. For example, Kenya's M-Pesa model initiated through a third party needs to be studied more carefully to examine its possible usage in India.

Once the business correspondent model becomes fairly successful, one can experiment with formation of Joint Liability Groups (JLG) in such urban regions. This can be started first with the women members through SHGs as during our survey we have observed the amiable disposition of women members (such as flower vendors) towards formal banks which trait was clearly absent in male members. JLG model can be experimented in the next step after the success of SHG and BC models.

Appendix

Table A7.1 Distribution of respondents with varying levels of financial exclusion, Bengaluru

	Percent
High level of inclusion	8.3
Marginally excluded	13.5
Severely excluded	33.8
Fully excluded	44.4
Total	100.0

Source Field survey

Table A7.2 Association between levels of financial inclusion and the following category, Bengaluru

Category	Financial inclusion 4 categories					
		Highly included	Marginally excluded	Severely excluded	Fully excluded	Total
Education	Illiterate	2.6	5.1	25.6	66.7	100
	Primary	5.7	15.1	34.0	45.3	100
	Secondary	11.4	22.9	42.9	22.9	100
	Graduate and above	50.0	–	33.3	16.7	100
	Total	8.3	13.5	33.8	44.4	100
	Chi-square tests	Pearson chi-square value = 30.90				
		Asymptotic significance = 0.0003				

(continued)

Table A7.2 (continued)

Category	Financial inclusion 4 categories					
		Highly included	Marginally excluded	Severely excluded	Fully excluded	Total
Type of business	Vegetables or Fruits	6.9	19.0	27.6	46.6	100
	Flower vendors	–	–	35.7	64.3	100
	Consumer goods of daily use	9.1	9.1	41.8	40.0	100
	Consumer durables (electronics and others)	50.0	25.0	25.0	–	100
	Eatery/tea vendor/others	–	50.0	–	50.0	100
	Total	8.3	13.5	33.8	44.4	100
	Chi-square tests	Pearson chi-square value = 22.06				
		Asymptotic significance = 0.037				
Daily profit range	Up to Rs. 350	–	9.5	14.3	76.2	100
	351–500	–	5.7	45.7	48.6	100
	501–750	12.0	20.0	36.0	32.0	100
	751–1000	21.9	15.6	25.0	37.5	100
	1001 and above	–	36.4	45.5	18.2	100
	Total	8.1	14.5	33.1	44.4	100
	Chi-square tests	Pearson chi-square value = 32.82				
		Asymptotic significance = 0.001				
Total family income	<=5000	–	–	–	100.0	100
	5001–10000	–	–	–	100.0	100
	10001–15000	5.1	7.7	30.8	56.4	100
	15001–25000	5.8	13.5	42.3	38.5	100
	>=25001	22.2	22.2	37.0	18.5	100
	Chi-square tests	Pearson chi-square value = 29.04				
		Asymptotic significance = 0.004				
Age	<25	–	–	66.7	33.3	100
	26-35	6.4	12.8	36.2	44.7	100
	36-45	14.3	8.6	28.6	48.6	100
	>46	6.3	18.8	33.3	41.7	100
	Total	8.3	13.5	33.8	44.4	100
	Chi-square tests	Pearson chi-square value = 5.87				
		Asymptotic significance = 0.753				
Type of shelter	Non regular shop	5.7	13.3	34.3	46.7	100
	Regular shop	17.9	14.3	32.1	35.7	100
	Total	8.3	13.5	33.8	44.4	100
	Chi-square tests	Pearson chi-square value = 4.58				
		Asymptotic significance = 0.204				

Table A7.3 Distribution of respondents according to the levels of their financial exclusion, Tumkur

	Percent
Fully included	12.1
Marginally excluded	14.3
Severely excluded	37.4
Fully excluded	36.3
Total	100.0

Source Field survey

Table A7.4 Association between levels of financial inclusion and the following category, Tumkur

Category	Financial inclusion 4 categories					
		Highly included	Marginally excluded	Severely excluded	Fully excluded	Total
Education	Illiterate	8.7	13	26.1	52.2	100
	Primary	13.8	3.4	27.6	55.2	100
	Secondary	8.3	22.2	55.6	13.9	100
	Graduate and above	50	50	0	0	100
	Total	11.1	14.4	37.8	36.7	100
	Chi-square tests	Pearson chi-square value = 24.43				
		Asymptotic significance = 0.003				
Type of business	Vegetables or fruits	18.2	12.1	27.3	42.4	100.0
	Flower vendors	–	–	–	100.0	100.0
	Consumer goods of daily use	11.4	5.7	60.0	22.9	100.0
	Consumer durables (electronics and Others)	–	43.8	18.8	37.5	100.0
	Eatery/ tea vendor/ others	–	–	100.0	–	100.0
	Total	11.1	14.4	37.8	36.7	100.0
	Chi-square tests	Pearson chi-square value = 34.23				
		Asymptotic significance = 0.0006				

(continued)

Table A7.4 (continued)

Category	Financial inclusion 4 categories					
		Highly included	Marginally excluded	Severely excluded	Fully excluded	Total
Daily profit range	Up to Rs. 350	12.5	12.5	25.0	50.0	100.0
	351 to 500	14.3	3.6	46.4	35.7	100.0
	501 to 750	8.7	26.1	30.4	34.8	100.0
	751 to 1000	21.4	21.4	35.7	21.4	100.0
	1001 and above	–	50.0	50.0		100.0
	Total	13.3	15.7	36.1	34.9	100.0
	Chi-square tests	Pearson chi-square value = 11.6325				
		Asymptotic significance = 0.475627				
Total family income	<=5000	–	–	11.1	88.9	100.0
	5001–10000	–	–	50.0	50.0	100.0
	10001–15000	13.5	11.5	40.4	34.6	100.0
	15001–25000	13.6	18.2	45.5	22.7	100.0
	>=25001	25.0	75.0			100.0
	Total	12.1	14.3	37.4	36.3	100.0
	Chi-square tests	Pearson chi-square value = 28.46				
		Asymptotic significance = 0.0047				
Age	<25			33.3	66.7	100.0
	26–35	18.2	4.5	45.5	31.8	100.0
	36–45	9.7	19.4	32.3	38.7	100.0
	>46	11.4	17.1	37.1	34.3	100.0
	Total	12.1	14.3	37.4	36.3	100.0
	Chi-square tests	Pearson chi-square value = 5.436038				
		Asymptotic significance = 0.794763				
Type of shelter	Non regular shop	11.4	6.8	31.8	50.0	100.0
	Regular shop	13.3	20.0	42.2	24.4	100.0
	Total	12.4	13.5	37.1	37.1	100.0
	Chi-square tests	Pearson chi-square value = 7.50				
		Asymptotic significance = 0.057				

Table A7.5 Reasons for not approaching bank and suggestion, Tumkur

Not approaching bank for initial capital	Percent
Investment was little—there was no necessity to seek bank and arranged through own savings	90.7
Arranged money with friends and relatives	28.9
Arranged money through money lender	3.1
Pre conceived notion and pessimistic attitude that bank will not give money	100
Tedious and strict procedures enforced by banks	40.2
No need as it is family business and started by elders	12.4
Approached bank-but rejected due to the current business falling under negative list of businesses	1.0
Not approaching bank for working capital	*Percent*
Approached bank-but rejected because the current business was under the negative list of businesses	3.1
Not aware that bank would provide loans for WC	22.7
Able to manage with daily turnover-business is small	56.7
Credit through whole sale traders is the most convenient way	63.9
Pessimistic attitude towards bank and hesitant to visit	72.2
Very tedious procedure in accessing the loan facility	59.8
Received loan from co-operative bank	19.6
Suggestions for improvement of bank services	*Percent*
Simplify Documentation Procedure to Open an account and procedurally should function like money lender (i.e., easily accessible at door step with	56.7
Easy access—needs more information	57.7
Waiting period to be minimized	10.3
Negative business should be given loan	39.2
Must be cordial towards street vendors	7.2
To ensure no corruption by bank officials and no frequent transfer of officials	5.2

Source Field survey

References

Chakrabarty KC (2013) Revving up the growth engine through financial inclusion, Address by Dr K C Chakrabarty, at the 32nd Skoch Summit, Mumbai, 6 June 2013 BIS Central Bankers Speeches, June 6

Rajeev Meenakshi, Vani BP, Veerashekharappa (2015) Financial inclusion through SHGs: Understanding quality and sustainability of SHGs in karnataka state. Monograph no. 40, Institute for Social and Economic Change, Bengaluru, India

Thorat U (2007) Financial inclusion—the Indian experience. RBI Monthly Bulletin, July, RBI

Thorat U (2010) Financial regulator and financial inclusion-working at cross purposes. BIS Rev 77

Chapter 8
Concluding Remarks and Policy Implications

This study examines accessibility and usage of banking services primarily by the economically weaker sections of the society who are self employed in urban regions, and hence in regular need of loan finance.

As revealed by macro level indicators relating to the banking sector published regularly by the Reserve Bank of India, there is wide disparity across states as also different regions in a state in the matter of availability and access of banking services. A regional analysis reveals that certain regions like the North-eastern and Eastern regions need special attention of the policy makers and administrators (Rajeev et al, 2015). Also the very low level of credit accounts in a nation where large sections of population are self employed and in need of finance on a regular basis, clearly indicates that poor are depending on informal sources of credit even for their production related needs. This is an area that needs due consideration.

Other developing nations across the globe can also learn important lessons from the Indian experience in this regard, i.e., that certain sections of population and regions need special attention in the context of financial inclusion drive. Further, India has been successful in initiating access to credit for the rural sector especially for the farmer class by making it mandatory for the banking sector to adhere to the priority sector lending norms. Under these norms, certain sectors like agriculture, small scale industries are designated as priority sector and the banks are required to direct 40% of credit to these sectors.

Our analysis of NSSO unit record (household level) data (AIDIS, 59th and 70th Rounds) reveals that the urban households face more problems while availing loans compared to their rural counterparts, and they generally get fewer loans from both formal and informal lending sources. It is also seen that poorer sections avail loans more from the informal sector at much higher rates of interest. Therefore, there is a need to improve credit delivery system for the urban poor especially the self-employed. It is also observed from our earlier analysis of NSSO data that the informal lenders generally collect interest accruals separately from borrowers leaving the principal amount untouched with the result the poor borrowers remain indebted even after paying several times the principal amount as interest. A comparison of interest rates charged by informal markets across households of different economic strata as well as states revealed that compared to the poorer households in

M. Rajeev and B.P. Vani, *Financial Access of the Urban Poor in India*,
SpringerBriefs in Economics, DOI 10.1007/978-81-322-3712-9_8

the states of Karnataka, Chhattisgarh and Madhya Pradesh, similarly placed households in the states of Punjab, Haryana and West Bengal get loans at lower interest rates from informal money lenders. However, for households with more than Rs. 1000 monthly per capita consumption expenditure, the difference was marginal or non-existent. Further, in states like Haryana and West Bengal, socially backward class households appear to have lower access to formal credit than the general category ones. In addition, the households headed by self employed women have much lower access to credit than the male headed households. Thus, there is a need to address the disparity in access found across different groups, regions, states etc. in order to devise policy measures to bring parity across such divisions.

These findings are of importance for other developing nations as well. Amongst the poorer sections, the lowest strata needs special attention. These are the people who need support from the state to access loans for funding their livelihood activities and hence the extent of financial exclusion within these categories needs to be highlighted. Gender disparity in financial access has been well recognised across the globe and many developing nations are trying to help women to access financial services through different schemes. Extension of financial services through women's self-help-groups, as has been quite successful in India and Bangladesh, can be adopted by the African nations to improve financial inclusion of the women. In Nigeria there is gold loan for women. In India too, gold loan-scheme is becoming quite popular, but one undesirable outcome of this, as noticed by the research group (see Rajeev and Vani 2016), is that the banks are now catering to the borrowers with gold on a priority basis. Thus, the poor borrowers who do not have gold to pledge, are getting left out. This is particularly so in case of farm loan given under gold security (Rajeev et al. 2016). This experience is of relevance to other developing nations as well. On the other hand, Morocco's experiment of providing insurance to women during the time of need say, during child birth, is an important model which can be profitably emulated by other developing countries including India.

Given the lower level of credit accessibility to the urban households in spite of having large number of banks branches (as revealed from the NSSO survey), this research decided to study the situation in a more focused manner. Of particular interest to us was the urban regions of the country, especially metropolitan cities such as Bengaluru where a large number of bank branches are concentrated. An interesting finding is that while the physical distance to the banks is minimal, the psychological barrier (antipathy) appears to be substantial for a large section of self-employed population though they are in need of funds on a regular basis. It was observed during our survey that in most instances this distance does not emerge from personal experiences but due to the overwhelming belief that banks are unapproachable. Given the presence of negative perception about banks, there is an urgent need to impart financial literacy to these groups that are in dire need of credit but are hesitant to approach banks. (For a detailed discussion on this topic, see Dr. Subbarao's speech dated March 4th, 2013, www.bis.org/review). Often, unfortunate experiences of a few spread through word of mouth and act as a general deterrent. For example, one of the traders who saved through pigmy collectors in banks had severe problem in withdrawing his money. Another trader also faced severe problem in withdrawing his own savings as he was unable to fill-in the requisite form. Further, when a few took loan from banks, the very fact that no collector was visiting them for loan (repayment) instalment collection regularly, eventually created a problem of repayment of the accumulated amount. Most of the respondents in our sample reported as having not approached banks for funds for starting business. The fear of consequences of default in repayment seems to have deterred several respondents from approaching banks for loan. Instead, many of the respondents took up only such business endeavours that could be done with their own savings, and for working capital needs they were found primarily dependent on the wholesale traders.

In Bengaluru as high as 45% of the respondents reported as not having ever approached formal financial institutions to meet any of their credit needs be it for their business or personal purposes. This figure is quite revealing as it shows the level of exclusion of people in urban regions who are spatially very close to banks, have financial resources (as per our survey findings) and also access various other financial intermediaries on a continuous basis. From this, one can well imagine the level of exclusion of the poor, such as slum dwellers in urban regions.

It is observed that the agents with better level of education and comparatively better economic status are the ones who have better access to the banking services. Thus, the agents (traders) who are perceived as incapable to pay higher rates of interest or access even informal credit, are generally shunned by the banking sector also. Age or experience of the person generally does not help him or her to have better access. Our survey also revealed that women have better faith in formal banking system than men even though both NSSO data and our survey show that currently their accessibility is lower than men. This category needs special attention of the policy makers.

A recent revisit to these markets for understanding the changes that may have occurred especially after the initiation of Jan Dhan Yojana showed that the situation has not improved much especially for the relatively poor traders. They remain excluded from the formal financial sector particularly for accessing credit. Thus, the lower strata continue to lack financial literacy and access and therefore need prioritised attention.

Unlike in the metros, in smaller towns like Tumkur, personalized initiatives of certain bank officials are found to have met with some success. Thanks to such initiatives taken by a UCO bank official, Tumkur sample shows that formal sector borrowings for meeting working capital needs have been increasing. Door to door service for repayment has also helped in getting the loan repaid.

Interviews that the researchers had with the bank officials have revealed their perception of the problem. As these urban branches deal generally with the educated and well to do clients, small borrowers often get crowded out due to high transaction costs involved in dealing with such small borrowers. Both the demand side and the supply side concede that there is a need to provide dedicated services to such small borrowers through business correspondent or self help group models. Such group based models can be experimented through women entrepreneurs to begin with. If it is found successful, the same can be extended to male groups also. But even for such group based models to work in urban areas, dedicated banking service channels are necessary.

Given the avowed policy objective of ensuring financial inclusion to these self employed small traders, it is necessary to provide tailor-made services to these clients. "MUDRA' is an important initiative of the current Government for the small entrepreneurs and the scheme has benefitted them to some extent. However, for the trading based self employed persons like the ones discussed in this research, most importantly, one bank office (kiosk) however small, should be in the market premises manned by at least one official, and collections should be ensured by sending business correspondents (BCs) to the clients' door step. Only then banking services will be of use to the small borrowers particularly in the urban regions of India.

In this context, it is also useful to have the views of the beneficiary groups. It is important to note that 100% of the respondent traders voiced the need to have a small bank office in the market itself, so that it is approachable to all the borrowers, large or small (Table 8.1). Thus the BC model discussed at length in the previous section could be a viable alternative. Further, if small savings facility and loan collection facilities are provided at doorstep through the BCs, better financial inclusion can be ensured. Such a mechanism will automatically bring about proper flow of information and cordiality between lenders and borrowers.

Currently, banking institutions like cooperative banks or Muslim lending societies are seen operating in certain market areas, though they are few and far between. But their reach is limited to the members who are usually mid size traders and not small borrowers. Discussions with the bank officials brought out a number of suggestions, some of which were included in the earlier sections and we add a few important suggestions below.

Promotion of self help groups (SHGs): Instead of targeting individual vendor or trader—who may not have a proper shop address or permanent residence—promotion of micro-finance activities through SHGs could be one solution. In this direction, a separate branch of Canara bank—Micro Finance branch dealing with Women Self Help Group (WSHGs) is already in operation in two cities, namely Bengaluru and Shimoga town. Other banks also have such specialized branches in certain locations. But the present coverage of these specialized branches is far short of demand, given the large number of such potential borrowers.

Scheme based loans: In addition, nationalized banks are authorized to lend money to the weaker section through the Differential Rate of interest (DAR) scheme. The objective of DAR is to improve the economic conditions of the weakest of the weaker

Table 8.1 Suggestions for improvement of bank services. *Source* Field Survey

	Percent
Should have a small office in the market premises. Simplify Documentation Procedure and procedurally should function like money lender (i.e., easily accessible at door step)	100
Easy access—needs more Information	44.4
Waiting period to be minimized	20.3
Must be cordial towards street vendors	27.8

sections of the community by providing financial assistance for engaging in productive and gainful activities at concessional rates of interest (of around 4%). Awareness about DAR scheme is currently very low among people and banks; banks should therefore make effort to popularize this scheme on a priority basis. Government has already issued guidelines to the banks pertaining to the DAR scheme for under developed districts (rural) in India. A similar scheme should be made applicable to urban poor also.

Business correspondent model: There is a need to make the Business Correspondent (BC) model more extensive to make financial inclusion successful. The RBI and other banks with large capital should take the initiative in this regard and more emphasis should be laid on promoting BC model in a more efficient and effective way in future. However, there is a need for concurrent evaluation of the scheme to suggest course correction as well as to put in place necessary checks and balances to make the BC model safe and transparent. There is also a need for credit-guarantee to hedge the savings of the self-employed poor traders. India can benefit from the experience of the developing nations that are currently using other business outlets or mobile technology for financial inclusion as discussed in the previous chapter. Another way to reduce the psychological barrier and motivate people to approach banks, as suggested by small business owners during our interviews, is by opening kiosk-based banking system within the market premises.

JLG or SHG Model: Once the business correspondent model becomes fairly successful one can experiment with formation of Joint Liability group model in such regions. Another finding of the survey is the ready acceptance by women of formal banking institutions and BC model of banking, which trait was absent in male members. Therefore, it is wise to start the experiment with the women traders. The JLG model can be experimented together with the BC model.

Mobile banking also has great potential in urban areas. Experience from Kenya is of relevance to India. Business transaction through mobile technology will revolutionize future banking. ADHAAR number (and data) which is used in India to provide a unique identification number to all people can be used by banks for know your customer (KYC) purposes and full proof identification of potential customers.

Urban cooperatives exist in India but the question is whether they really reach the poorest among the self employed. In this respect, Rwandan experiment discussed in detail in the previous chapter could be of great value to India and other developing nations.

If some of the steps suggested above are accepted and made operational, financial exclusion of the self employed poor in the urban regions can be reduced to a great extent.

References

Rajeev Meenakshi, Vani BP, Veerashekharappa (2015) Financial inclusion through SHGs: Understanding quality and sustainability of SHGs in karnataka state. Monograph no. 40, Institute for Social and Economic Change, Bengaluru, India

Rajeev Meenakshi and Vani B P (2016) Interest Subvention Related to Agriculture Credit In Karnataka, Project Report No. CESP/RBI/128, Institute for Social and Economic Change, Bengaluru, India

FSC
www.fsc.org
MIX
Papier | Fördert gute Waldnutzung
FSC® C083411

Kolibri 360 GmbH
Ferdinand-Jühlke-Straße 7
99095 Erfurt, Deutschland
produktsicherheit@kolibri360.de